WATER CRISIS:
Ending the Policy Drought

*This book has been published under
the auspices of the Cato Institute.*

WATER CRISIS:
Ending the Policy Drought

TERRY L. ANDERSON

The Johns Hopkins University Press
Baltimore and London

Printed in the United States of America.

The Johns Hopkins University Press, Baltimore, Maryland 21218
The Johns Hopkins Press Ltd., London

LC 83-48046
ISBN 0-8018-3087-7
ISBN 0-8018-3088-5 pbk

CONTENTS

ACKNOWLEDGMENTS

The author wishes to thank the Cato Institute for its support and encouragement for the writing of this monograph. Without such support, our understanding of markets and their potential for solving important social problems would be significantly less.

This would also be true of the support received from the Center for Political Economy and Natural Resources. Because of the facilities and personnel at the Center, this book is a much better product. John Baden provided valuable ideas and feedback. Marianne Keddington, Center editor, confronted me with hundreds of "not clears," which I hope have become clear in the process. Finally, I must thank the Noble Foundation and the Scaife Family Charitable Trust, which have provided general financial support for the Center and made possible my contact with John and Marianne.

The authors of chapters in *Water Rights: Scarce Resource Allocation, Bureaucracy, and the Environment,* Terry L. Anderson, ed. (Cambridge, Mass.: Ballinger Press and the Pacific Institute, 1983) also deserve much credit. Many of their ideas form the foundations for arguments presented here. The reader desiring more technical and detailed analysis is referred to that book. In particular I thank Oscar Burt, Del Gardner, Jim Huffman, Ron Johnson, and Rod Smith for their valuable insights into water institutions.

To Sarah and Peter,
may they always respect
the rights of others

FOREWORD

Terry Anderson provides an informative, provocative, and imaginative analysis of the problems of water "shortage" and of the property rights to water. Both those who accept his conclusions and those who question or criticize his analysis will be impressed with its comprehensiveness, its neatly logical structure, and its clarity of exposition.

Water is vital to human life and welfare everywhere in the world, but especially so in the western United States. The book is about water in the West and particularly about the Pacific Coast and Northwest. Concepts about legal rights to water in this region, like legal concepts about land, were imported from other parts of the United States and from other countries. The initial concepts were based on inadequate knowledge of hydrology, economics, and law, and have changed as natural resource use has developed in the West.

The concept of appropriation of water was developed by miners who needed dependable rights to use water, which they diverted from streams for use elsewhere. Anderson feels that the appropriation doctrine was well adapted to the times and circumstances. As the economic development of the West proceeded, available water supplies were used more fully, creating competition for the available water. This has forced the development of new concepts as well as new investments to augment available supplies.

Water users and competitors increasingly turned their efforts toward greater governmental controls over water rights and water use and toward greater governmental involvement in water development projects. This necessarily involved rejection or abandonment of the private market for water. Anderson documents the obstacles that arise when water use is shifted from one kind of use to another or from one area of use to another. Such obstacles exist especially for shifts to environmental and recreational uses but are almost equally serious for shifts within kinds or areas of commercial water use. Agriculture is, of course, the biggest user, and irrigation water rights are almost frozen to today's farms.

As a result of the development of water rights, there exists today in the West a rigid pattern of rights, which if understandable at all, is so only in terms of its history. The system of rights used today arose in a much earlier time. Efforts to transfer water from one area to another or from one use to another are difficult, time-consuming, and uncertain in outcome. The situation has been exacerbated by extensive federal water development projects, with water priced at absurdly low levels and tied to particular tracts of farmland. But many, perhaps most, private users of water intuitively or subconsciously price their water far below its full value in alternative uses because there is no ready market for the transfer of water rights, and hence, users lack the information about water values that a competitive market could provide. Low prices for water encourage waste. The resulting "scarcity" and "crisis" are strictly manmade, institutional rather than hydrologic or engineering in character.

Anderson carefully develops the logical arguments for a private market in water rights and describes the advantages of such a market. Of course, in doing so, he is following lines of reasoning developed by many other economists, either generally, or specifically for water. Perhaps his greatest contribution is his thoughtful and imaginative proposals for implementation of programs for the development of such a private market in water rights. Basically, he says we should return to the original concept of the appropriation doctrine which permitted transfers of water from one area, one use, and one owner to another, relatively freely and without many governmental restrictions. He describes in some detail how this might work and anticipates some of the objections that will be raised.

Critics and defenders of the status quo may argue that Anderson is not critical enough in his arguments for a private market in water rights and that he underestimates the problems of implementing such a market. It is true that he does not fully face up to the reasons why many interests in the West support the present system, including the federal water development programs which have become increasingly expensive and unproductive. Nevertheless, Anderson's analysis deserves attention and respect. An early reform of the present rigid and wasteful system is unlikely and perhaps we will never see full reform. But Anderson shows most convincingly that water shortages in the West exist only because we collectively have created them.

MARION CLAWSON
Resources for the Future

xii

I. The Coming Water Crisis

"Drought, waste and pollution threaten a water shortage whose impact may rival the energy crisis," warns a *Newsweek* cover story.[1] Photographs of dried-up water supplies, sinkholes the size of football fields, rivers that catch fire, and huge sprinkler irrigation systems are used to illustrate the growing water crisis. As memories of the dust bowl linger and as water shortages become more common, we are forced to wonder: Are we running out of water?

The Evidence

With most natural resources, concern over future availability is based on an inventory view. This view compares existing or predicted quantities of resource availability with predicted consumption patterns. Whenever rising rates of consumption collide with declining availability, a crisis is predicted. Many general studies of resource use have concluded that both renewable and nonrenewable resources are being used at an alarming rate. *The Limits to Growth* study, for example, was bold enough to pinpoint a year early in the next century when our growing consumption of resources will collide with our dwindling supplies.[2] *The Global 2000 Report*, a similar study commissioned by the Carter administration, concluded that

> if present trends continue, the world in 2000 will be more crowded, more polluted, less stable ecologically, and more vulnerable to disruption than the world we live in now. Serious stresses involving population, resources, and environment are clearly visible ahead.[3]

These same conclusions also have been reached regarding the availability of water. The U.S. Water Resources Council has estimated the availability of the nation's water resources and concluded that

---

[1]"The Browning of America," *Newsweek*, February 23, 1981, pp. 26–37.

[2]Donella H. Meadows, Denis L. Meadows, Jorgen Randers, and William W. Behens III, *The Limits to Growth* (New York: Potomac Association, 1972).

[3]Council on Environmental Quality (CEQ), *The Global 2000 Report to the President*, vol. 1 (Washington, D.C.: Government Printing Office, 1980), p. 1.

on the average, about 40,000 bgd (billion gallons per day) of water passes over the coterminous United States in the form of water vapor. Of this, approximately 10 per cent (about 4,200 bgd) is precipitated as rainfall, snow, sleet, or hail. The remainder continues in atmospheric suspension. Of the 4,200 bgd . . . about 2/3 (2,750 bgd) is evaporated immediately from the wet surfaces or transpired by vegetation. The remaining 1,450 bgd accumulates in ground or surface storage; flows to the oceans, the Gulf of Mexico or across the Nation's boundaries; is consumptively used; or is evaporated from reservoirs.[4]

Since the beginning of the 20th century, total water withdrawals have risen continuously, with total water consumption increasing dramatically since 1960 (see table 1). Water consumed as a percentage of water withdrawn rose between 1960 and 1975. By 1975, there were 393 billion gallons per day (bgd) being withdrawn from surface and groundwater sources in the coterminous United States and 107 bgd were being consumed. While it might appear that this would leave plenty of water, some of it must be left to flow into Canada and Mexico. Furthermore, locational demands for water do not always coincide with supplies. Future energy development in the West, for example, will consume large quantities of water in an area where already too much water is used.

Table 1

WATER WITHDRAWALS AND CONSUMPTION, 1960–2000, IN BILLIONS OF GALLONS PER DAY

Year	Total Water Withdrawals	Total Consumptive Use
1960	270	61
1965	336	77
1970	370	88
1975	393	107
1985	422	121
2000	425	135

SOURCE: National Water Commission, *Water Policies for the Future,* Final Report (Washington, D.C.: Government Printing Office, 1973), p. 7; and U.S. Water Resources Council, *The Nation's Water Resources,* vol. 1 (Washington, D.C.: Government Printing Office, 1978), p. 29.

[4]U.S. Water Resources Council, *The Nation's Water Resources, 1975–2000* (Washington, D.C.: Government Printing Office, 1978), p. 12.

By the turn of the next century water shortages are likely to become more widespread. The Water Resources Council does predict that withdrawals from streams will decrease by 9 percent between 1975 and 2000. During the same period, however, consumption of fresh water is expected to increase by almost 27 percent. Some of the difference will be made up from groundwater sources and some from "more efficient use of water as a result of conservation efforts and better technology in recycling and similar procedures."[5] Despite these predictions of improved efficiency, the Water Resources Council estimates that "seventeen subregions have or will have a serious problem of inadequate surface-water supply by the year 2000."[6]

The problem is even worse if groundwater is considered separately. Approximately 82 bgd are currently being withdrawn from groundwater basins, and only 61 bgd are flowing back in. Groundwater mining is causing subsidence, salt water intrusion, higher pumping costs, and general alarm about the future of groundwater supplies. In some areas, groundwater levels are declining at a rate of "7 to 10 feet per year. Extensive groundwater overdraft is occurring in 8 of the 106 subregions. Moderate groundwater overdraft is occurring in an additional 30 subregions."[7]

Pollution of both surface and groundwater may also be increasing. In 1975, the Water Resources Council was optimistic that "water-quality conditions will be improved substantially. With the emphasis on more intensive use and reuse of available supplies, improvement of quality should become an important facet of water-management procedures."[8] Budget cutbacks for most federal agencies, including the Environmental Protection Agency, however, have prompted many people to question whether environmental quality will improve in the future.

The Global 2000 study concluded that "pollution, GNP, and resource projections all imply rapidly increasing demands for fresh water. Increases of at least 200-300 percent in world water withdrawals are expected over the 1975–2000 period."[9] The increased demand is based largely on population growth, which is expected to "cause demands for water to at least double relative to 1971 in nearly half of the countries of the

[5]Ibid., p. 2.
[6]Ibid.
[7]Ibid.
[8]Ibid., p. 78.
[9]CEQ, p. 26.

3

world."[10] This means that in the year 2000 the western half of the United States as well as the area from Texas to Maryland will have moved from a 1971 water availability of more than 10,000 cubic meters per person to between 5,000 and 10,000 cubic meters of water per person. The rest of the country will experience a decline from 5,000 to 10,000 cubic meters to 1,000 to 5,000 cubic meters. Water for increased food production, new energy production, conventional power generation, and other industrial needs are predicted to aggravate water shortages. The rising cost of energy is expected to "adversely effect the economics of many water development projects, and may reduce the amount of water available for a variety of uses. Irrigation, which usually requires large amounts of energy for pumping, may be particularly affected."[11] The bottom line is that unless we change our ways, a crisis is inevitable.

What Causes a Crisis?

It is true that "the energy crisis and the water shortage are inextricably linked,"[12] but the connection is probably more subtle than most people understand. Rising energy prices have made supplying water more costly, but the general link between energy and water is more directly related to the extent to which prices are allowed to influence demand and supply. In economic terms, a crisis exists when the quantity demanded is greater than the quantity available and when there is little time to adjust either of them. This is exactly what the energy crisis was and what the water crisis is likely to be. The question is, why does quantity demanded not equal quantity supplied?

The 1970s taught us an important lesson: When the government keeps fuel prices below market-clearing levels, shortages inevitably follow. Further, once shortages occur and as price controls block normal market mechanisms, the government is forced into the business of allocating scarce supplies. Federal price controls for gasoline and the blundering attempts to allocate gasoline in 1974 and 1979 had social costs that far exceeded the limited relief provided to gasoline purchasers. Experience around the world has demonstrated over and over again that the only successful way to avoid fuel shortages is to rely on free-market pricing and allocation.[13]

[10]Ibid.

[11]Ibid., pp. 26–27.

[12]"The Browning of America," p. 27.

[13]Robert E. Hall and Robert S. Pindyck, "What to Do When Energy Prices Rise Again," *The Public Interest* 65 (Fall 1981): 68.

The same circumstances are causing problems with water. Water prices have been kept below market-clearing levels, and the inevitable shortages have followed. The government has responded by attempting to constrain demand, ration water, and increase the available supply. Except in isolated cases where shortages have been caused by drought and where a cooperative community spirit has developed, efforts to ration water have not been successful. Increased water supplies have only been possible through the construction of massive water projects, which have dammed many of our free-flowing rivers and built thousands of miles of aqueducts. These projects have been extremely costly, and it is questionable whether funds for them will continue to be available. Without a price mechanism operating on water supply and demand, crisis situations will continue to arise.

Could Markets Do Better?

In arguing that the price mechanism has not been allowed to work for allocating water there is the implicit assumption that price rationing could help resolve the water crisis. At higher prices people tend to consume less of a commodity and search for alternative means of achieving their desired ends. Water is no exception. The data in table 2 suggest that both producers and consumers have technologies available to them that would allow different patterns of water consumption. These data also suggest that the pattern of water use will vary considerably among regions, depending on price and value.

The actual responsiveness of water consumption to price changes will vary among regions with the variations depending on such variables as income and precipitation. In their study of six subregions of the United States, Bruce Beattie and Henry Foster found that a 10 percent increase in the price of water would produce between a 3.75 and 12.63 percent decrease in water consumption. The Northern California and Pacific Northwest region, with its abundant rainfall, was the most responsive, and the arid Southwest region was the least responsive. While these estimates may suggest that higher water prices could reduce consumption, it must be noted that in 57 percent of the 23 cities studied real water prices declined between 1960 and 1976. Only three cities had real water rate increases of more than one dollar per 1,000 cubic feet.[14] Beattie and Foster concluded that

> the water utility industry has done a good job for consumers. Unfor-

[14]Bruce R. Beattie and H. S. Foster Jr., "Can Prices Tame the Inflationary Tiger?," *Journal of the American Water Works Association* 72 (August 1980): 444–45.

Table 2

Variance in Industrial Unit Water Withdrawal

| | Draft (in gallons) | | |
Product or User and Unit	Maximum	Typical	Minimum
Steam-electric power (kw-h.)	170	80	1.32
Petroleum refining (gallon of crude oil)	44.5	18.3	1.73
Steel (finished ton)	65,000	40,000	1,400
Soaps, edible oils (pound)	7.5	—	1.57
Carbon black (pound)	14	4	0.25
Natural rubber (pound)	6	—	2.54
Butadiene (pound)	305	160	13
Glass containers (ton)	667	—	118
Automobiles (per car)	16,000	—	12,000
Trucks, buses (per unit)	20,000	—	15,000

SOURCE: H. E. Hudson and Janet Abu-Lughod, "Water Requirements," *Water for Industry,* Jack B. Graham and Meredith F. Burrill, eds. Publication no. 45 (Washington, D.C.: American Association for the Advancement of Science, 1956), pp. 19–21.

> tunately, because of this good job water users have adjusted their way of life so that needs for water are great. . . . Thus, how much water consumers need depends not only on willingness and ability to pay, but most importantly on the real price charged. If it is a lot, only a modest amount of water is needed. If the charge is a little, a lot is needed. The choice is largely up to the water utility industry.[15]

Similar data suggest that the agricultural sector demand for water is also price-responsive. Demand responsiveness varies by crop, of course, but some aggregate estimates for California show that a 10 percent increase in price would bring about a 6.5 percent decrease in water consumption. The same price increase would cause an overall average decrease of 3.7 percent for the 17 Western states. Estimates for homogeneous production areas in California show that at a price of $17, a 10 percent increase in price would yield a 20 percent decrease in water use.[16] These relatively high elasticities indicate that farmers in homogeneous production areas

[15]Ibid., p. 445.

[16]B. Delworth Gardner, "Water Pricing and Rent Seeking in California Agriculture," in *Water Rights: Scarce Resource Allocation, Bureaucracy, and the Environment,* Terry Anderson, ed. (Cambridge, Mass.: Ballinger Press, 1983).

would not be using all the water DWR [the California Department of Water Resources] was planning to send them—at the price DWR was planning to charge. . . . the marginal cost of water to the farmer would have to be reduced between $4 and $6 per acre-foot (from a contractual price of $14.70 per acre-foot in one HPA [homogeneous production area] and $16.36 in the other) before DWR's projected 1½ million acres would be brought into production.[17]

The implications are significant. If water prices are kept low, more demands will be placed on water resources. The additional water use will be subject to diminishing returns—the last units consumed will generate much less value than the first. What is seen as waste or inefficient water use in rural and urban areas is simply the users' rational response to low water prices. When water for lawns is left to run into storm gutters or when irrigation water erodes the field without reaching the roots of the plant, it is easy to say that users are being wasteful. But users can only afford to be wasteful when water is cheap. In agriculture, if water carried a higher price, it is likely that less water would be applied to any given crop, that different irrigation technology or water application practices would be used, and that different cropping patterns might appear.

Research conducted at the University of California suggests that reduced water application would decrease most crop yields but that at higher water prices such reductions would be economical. Flood irrigation techniques conserve on labor but use large amounts of water. With high water prices, it makes sense to substitute labor and capital for water and to use drip irrigation or similar techniques. Trimble Hedges provided similar evidence in a simulation of a 640-acre farm in Yolo County, California.[18] Hedges showed that the optimal cropping pattern at a zero water price would call for 150 acres each of tomatoes, sugar beets, and wheat; 47 acres of alfalfa; 65 acres of beans; and 38 acres of safflower. If the water price were increased to $13.50 per acre foot, alfalfa acreage would drop out and safflower acreage, a crop that uses less water, would expand. The point is that many choices are available to water consumers and they will respond rationally to water prices.

Higher water prices will also reduce the need to build costly supply

[17]Ibid.

[18]Trimble R. Hedges, *Water Supplies and Costs in Relation to Farm Resource Decisions and Profits on Sacramento Valley Farms*, Report no. 322 (Berkeley, Calif.: Gianinni Foundation, June 1977).

projects. Higher water prices in Southern California would greatly reduce the incentives for constructing the Peripheral Canal and other costly delivery systems, the damming of free-flowing streams, and the battles over water rights. Higher water prices would also encourage private, profit-making firms to enter the water supply industry, taking the burden off the public treasury. If the price mechanism is allowed to operate, demand could be reduced, supply could be increased, and the water crisis could follow the energy crisis into memory.

What Lies Ahead?

Institutions that currently govern water allocation do not promote market solutions to water problems. But for these institutions and policies to change, a new perspective on the role of information and incentives is necessary. The new resource economics, described in chapter II, provides this perspective. Rather than following the traditional economic approach that calls for better cost-benefit analyses and better bureaucrats, the new resource economics calls for a closer look at the rules of the game that determine incentives.

An examination of the history of water institutions reveals that an efficient set of property rights evolved in the American West during the last half of the 19th century and that entrepreneurs set up projects for storing and delivering water. By early in the 20th century, however, the basis for a private, market solution to water allocation, for all practical purposes, had been eroded. Chapter III details the evolution of water institutions, and chapter IV discusses how court interpretations eroded the doctrine of prior appropriations and how public reclamation projects discouraged private investment. If we are to solve the water crisis, it is necessary to discover how existing institutions must change. Chapter V shows that by removing restrictions on the transfer of surface water rights, markets could be used to a greater extent to promote efficient allocation. In chapter VI we see how instream uses can also be left more to market forces if restrictions on ownership for instream purposes are eliminated. Finally, chapter VII looks at how groundwater, which has traditionally been considered a common pool resource, can be bought and sold in markets if rights to stocks and flows are established.

By considering isolated examples of market solutions to water allocation problems, perhaps the collective institutions that dominate can be replaced with private institutions that promote efficiency and individual freedom. It is unlikely that the institutions necessary for a well-functioning market can be imposed through a central government.

The history of water rights suggests that order, not lawlessness, was promoted in the mining camps of the American West.[19] To be sure, collective action played a part in the evolutionary process, but that action was more decentralized and based more on a sense of natural rights than are current legislative solutions. If a market solution to the water crisis is to be achieved, the current morass of legislative and administrative rules will have to be replaced. A way must be found to channel collective action into the definition and enforcement of private property rights.

Since the points emphasized in this book follow closely the work of Jack Hirshleifer, James De Haven, and Jerome Milliman, it is appropriate to consider their view of decentralization:

> Other things being equal, we prefer local to state authority, state to federal—and private decision-making (the extreme of decentralization) to any of these. Our fundamental reason for this preference is the belief that the cause of human liberty is best served by a minimum of government compulsion and that, if compulsion is necessary, local and decentralized authority is more acceptable than dictation from a remote centralized source of power. This is an "extra market value" for which we at least would be willing to make some sacrifices in terms of loss of economic efficiency. . . . Even on grounds of efficiency, however, we have some faith that, the more nearly the costs and benefits of water projects are brought home to those who make decisions, the more correct those decisions are likely to be—a consideration which argues for decentralization in practice.[20]

The lack of well-defined and enforced property rights for many aspects of water has promoted centralized decisions on water use. All levels of government have become involved in water allocation, and the federal government particularly has seen its role expand since the turn of the century. To reverse this trend, private rights must be established if individuals acting in a market are to determine water allocation. This book describes how such rights can be formed to encourage efficiency in a society of free and responsible individuals.

[19]Terry L. Anderson and P. J. Hill, "An American Experiment in Anarcho-Capitalism: The *Not* So Wild, Wild West," *Journal of Libertarian Studies* 3 (1979): 9–30.

[20]Jack Hirshleifer, James C. De Haven, and Jerome W. Milliman, *Water Supply: Economics, Technology, Policy* (Chicago: University of Chicago Press, 1960), pp. 361–62.

II. The New Resource Economics: An Analytical Framework

Environmentalists, fiscal conservatives, and individuals who place a high value on freedom. Sound like strange bedfellows? Certainly most environmental and natural resource policies have forced these groups to hold conflicting positions, but a growing number of people are beginning to believe that they could join together to realize their diverse goals. In terms of the newly emerging resource economics paradigm, the potential for such an alliance is not startling. Two recent editorials support this contention by suggesting that environmentalists are beginning to understand the basis for and the power of this coalition.

Lawrence Burke, editor-in-chief of *Outside* magazine, argued in a 1982 editorial that a freely functioning energy market could eliminate many environmentally degrading projects.[1] Burke pointed out that the synfuels program, which would "lay waste to the western United States," received its momentum from government subsidies to private firms and price regulations. With the decontrol of oil prices, consumption declined and supplies increased, inducing private companies to back away from the program. Burke argued that the environmental problems associated with synfuels would not have occurred had there been free markets for petroleum, a position consistent with the newly emerging paradigm.

The second editorial surfaced after Proposition 9, the Peripheral Canal Bill, was defeated in California. Thomas Graff, General Counsel for the Environmental Defense Fund, heralded the defeat, but then went on to ask: "What now? Will it be development without environmental protection as some have threatened? Or has all future water-project development been choked off by the new conservationist-conservative alliance . . .?"[2] Graff stated that for California water policy to be environmentally and economically sound three reforms were necessary: legal and institutional barriers to voluntary sale and purchase

---

[1]Lawrence Burke, "Free Market Environmentalism," *Outside* (June-July 1982), p. 6.

[2]Thomas J. Graff, "Future Water Plans Need a Trickle-Up Economizing," *Los Angeles Times*, June 14, 1982, p. V-2.

of water rights must be eliminated; public investment must only be committed to lower-cost projects; and water pricing must be reformed so consumers will face the true cost of the resources they use.

Why is this alliance emerging and what are its implications for solving the water crisis? These questions will be addressed in this chapter. First, however, the new resource economics must be placed in context. In order to do this, it is necessary to examine the traditional economic approach to formulating water policy, outlining its contributions to current practices and dissecting its flaws.

Critique of the Traditional Approach

The late 1800s formed the watershed in classical and neoclassical economics by teaching us that economic decisions involve a comparison of marginal benefits with marginal costs. Until sufficient action has been taken to equate the two, optimization cannot be attained. Once this principle is mastered, it becomes clear that incremental adjustments are possible and that neither demand nor supply is perfectly inelastic. More recently, Harold Barnett and Chandler Morse drove this point home by demonstrating that substitution holds the key to mitigating the impacts of resource scarcity.[3] Their data show that most resources have gotten *less* scarce because people have found substitutes. For example, when whale oil became more expensive in the late 19th century, people substituted less expensive fuels; and, as discussed in chapter I, rising water prices have induced consumers to use less water by giving them incentives to switch to less expensive alternatives.

In recognizing that these incremental adjustments take place in an uncertain world where only imperfect information is available, economists have extended their models to incorporate these problems. The extension has taken basically two courses. First, following marginal analysis, the economics of information suggests that there is an optimal amount of search put into collecting information. Information is produced like any other good; and since a decision-maker does not have an infinite amount of free information available to him, actual equilibrium results will differ from those derived from textbook models. Second, economists were led to consider how expectations are formed and how risk preferences affect decisions. Again, the emphasis has been on marginal analysis and on equilibrium that depends on the formation of rational expectations.

[3]Harold J. Barnett and Chandler Morse, *Scarcity and Growth* (Baltimore: Johns Hopkins University Press, 1963).

Since most decisions involve some degree of allocation over time, the time preference of individuals and the time productivity of resources are crucial for determining intertemporal allocation. In the 1930s, Harold Hotelling made economists wary of notions such as maximum sustained yield.[4] Economists also began to realize that natural resources, like other assets, have prices related to the discount rate. The specific application of intertemporal choice to water resources has dramatically changed how economists look at exhaustible and renewable resources.

Application of the principles of marginal analysis, information and uncertainty, and interest theory to water resources has led many economists to conclude that collective action is often necessary. When private costs are less than social costs or when private benefits are less than social benefits, an externality exists and market failure results; that is, when private and social rates of return diverge, private decision-makers will not allocate water optimally. The existence of such externalities will depend on whether property rights are well-defined, enforced, and transferable. Most economic analyses of water allocation have concluded that these conditions cannot be met. It is argued, for example, that groundwater is a common pool resource. When individual pumpers extract the resource from a basin, they do not take into account the impact their actions might have on other users' pumping costs or on the future value of water. Most natural resource economists contend that common pool problems like this are pervasive and that, therefore, governmental intervention is necessary.

Since the existence of market failure suggests possible gains from collective action, much economic research has focused on how governmental intervention can improve efficiency. Leading the charge is cost-benefit analysis. Volumes have been written on this subject and on its application to water resources. Economists have developed ingenious sampling and statistical techniques for obtaining necessary data. As a result, all governmental agencies involved in water resource allocation are engaged in some form of cost-benefit analysis. Their efforts, however, are complicated by the fact that the value derived from water resources and the opportunity costs associated with their use accrue over time. Cost-benefit analysis can be an effective tool only if analysts can accurately predict available alternatives for supply and demand. In the absence of markets, this task is difficult enough when analysts are considering current circumstances, when information is relatively

[4]Harold Hotelling, "The Economics of Exhaustible Resources," *Journal of Political Economy* 39 (1931): 137–75.

abundant. The crystal ball becomes cloudy when periods 5, 10, or 20 years into the future must be considered.

Another complication arises as analysts realize that benefits or costs that accrue today have a higher value than those that accrue in the future; that is, future benefits and costs must be discounted to obtain their present value. Cost-benefit analysts continually wrestle with choosing the appropriate discount rate, and there is no simple way to choose. Public decision-makers are confronted with a wide range of possible discount rates and with arguments that the discount rate for society is different from that for private individuals. The choice is extremely important, since it will influence cost-benefit levels significantly. High discount rates will give more weight to benefits and costs in the present, and low discount rates will give relatively more weight to benefits and costs in the future. In a market setting, with efficient property rights, those who reap benefits or bear costs choose discount rates that are consistent with their preferences and with the opportunity costs of alternative investments. The choice will also include some component for the risks assessed by the individual decision-maker.

Traditional resource economists have assumed that scientific managers will apply cost-benefit analysis and the tools of neoclassical economics to obtain the optimal allocation of resources. Since the scientific manager is *not* motivated by profit or self-interest, it is *hoped* or *assumed* that he will apply the theory and methods impartially and efficiently to accomplish his agency's goals. The scientific manager is supposed to be like the economist, "always *analytical*. . . . Always, the economist's reasoning is analytical framework . . . his data, and his conclusions are exposed forthrightly to the examination and criticism of others. In these ways, *scientific objectivity* is actively sought. Polemics, pamphleteering and outright advocacy are left to others, or to the economist in his nonprofessional role as a citizen and a human being."[5] But public managers make decisions on the allocation and use of resources in a political arena where polemics, pamphleteering, and advocacy are part of the game.

When managers have not objectively responded to resource problems, traditional resource economists have proposed perfecting bureaucracy. For example, Robert Haveman has argued that the "use of natural and environmental resources is dominated by market failures"[6]

[5]Alan Randall, *Resource Economics* (Columbus, Ohio: Grid Publishing, 1981), p. 36.

[6]Robert H. Haveman, "Efficiency and Equity in Natural Resource and Environmental Policy," *American Journal of Agricultural Economics* 55 (1973): 868.

and that policymakers have responded to these failures by adopting rule-making/enforcement policy strategies, engaging in public investment programs, and developing policies on preservation/developmental alternatives.[7] Since policymakers have not always remained "scientifically objective," Haveman's reforms call for a National Commission on User Charge and Beneficiary Cost-Sharing and an Office of Policy Evaluation and Analysis, which will supposedly improve the efficiency of government.[8]

Those who call for such solutions fail to recognize that the same incentives that led to the problem will also exist in the proposed bureaucratic alternatives. What reason is there to believe that an Office of Policy Evaluation and Analysis with substantial staff capability would be any more scientifically objective? Even if it were, what reason is there to believe that bureaucratic decision-makers would apply their scientifically objective studies to policy?

The traditional approach taken by resource economists has taught us that market failure is pervasive in water allocation and that cost-benefit analysis applied by scientific, objective managers can improve on the failures. Building on marginal analysis, the neoclassical paradigm has lent itself well to mathematical modeling and statistical estimation, and many believe that this rigorous approach to economics allows shadow prices to be derived and used in lieu of actual market processes. Governmental agencies, such as the Bureau of Reclamation, the Office of Water Resources and Technology, the Army Corps of Engineers, and the Forest Service, are enamoured with building models that generate sophisticated mathematical and statistical results designed to improve resource management. The assumption is that given sufficient data and sophisticated computers, it is possible to produce wise and efficient management plans.

The FORPLAN model used by the Forest Service provides a state-of-the-art example of model building. Forest economist Richard Behan has concluded that this model and the current planning process is

> as close to the classic, rational and comprehensive model, and as close to perfection, as human imagination can design and implement. . . . RPA/NFMA [Resource Planning Act and National Forest Management Act] mandates with the force of law that forest plans can be rational, comprehensive, and essentially perfect. We have adopted an idealized

[7]Ibid., p. 870.
[8]Ibid., p. 876.

planning process and blessed it with all the force and power and rigor of statutes that a law-based society can muster.[9]

In spite of such modeling efforts, water allocation in particular and public resource management in general seem destined for a crisis.

In contrast to traditional approaches, the new resource economics (NRE) focuses on the information and incentives that result from market and nonmarket institutions. Anthony Fisher has captured the essence of why NRE is critical of collective allocation:

> We have already abandoned the assumption of a complete set of competitive markets. . . . But, if we now similarly abandon the notion of a perfect planner, it is not clear, in my judgment, that the government will do any better. Apart from the question of the planner's motivation to behave in the way assumed in our models, to allocate resources efficiently, there is the question of his ability to do so.[10]

Because cost-benefit analysis and efficiency criteria pay little attention to the institutions that structure and provide information and incentives, resource economists often puzzle over why efficiency implications are not more widely incorporated into policy formulation. Such concepts are useful in the private sector because decision-makers have information in the form of market prices and the incentives to act on that information. In the public sector, neither of these conditions hold. The "products" that are generated from publicly owned resources are, for the most part, zero-priced. Because there are no markets, the public resource manager is forced to make marginal comparisons without the benefit of information contained in prices. The lack of economic information forces the public manager to make trade-offs between alternative resource uses in terms of political currencies; these currencies, at best, provide distorted measures of value.

Public resource managers have an additional problem: The incentive structure in the public sector is quite different from that in the private sector. In the private sector, decision-makers are residual claimants, so someone receives the residual that is left after all costs have been paid.[11] The owner, or residual claimant, has an incentive to find good infor-

[9]Richard W. Behan, "RPA/NFMA—Time to Punt," *Journal of Forestry* 79 (December 1981): 802.

[10]Anthony C. Fisher, *Resource and Environmental Economics* (Cambridge: Cambridge University Press, 1981), p. 54.

[11]Armen A. Alchian and Harold Demsetz, "Production, Information Costs, and Economic Organization," *American Economic Review* 62 (1972): 777–95.

mation and use it to improve efficiency, which in turn enhances the residual claim. In the public sector, however, there is no residual claimant. The rewards for state water engineers do not depend on maximizing the net value of water resources. While there is no consensus in the economics literature on what is maximized by bureaucrats, most agree that efficiency is not the decision-maker's main goal. If a public resource manager were to pursue efficiency, it would have to be because he was honest and sincerely interested in the public interest, not because he was self-interested.

Because information and incentives have not been emphasized by traditional resource economists, the standard paradigm can be improved on by incorporating elements of property rights, public choice, and Austrian economics. The property rights approach brings into focus the relationship between institutions and incentives. Public choice draws attention to the incentives of bureaucrats and public officials and examines the likelihood of collective action achieving efficiency or equity. The production and dissemination of information are the key to Austrian economics, which holds that the entrepreneur is at the heart of all decisions. While the incorporation of these three elements is by no means complete, it is being extended to make natural resource economics more realistic. What follows is a brief synthesis of that new way of thinking.

The New Resource Economics

The new resource economics paradigm begins with the individual—especially the entrepreneur. Following marginal analysis, entrepreneurs search for situations where marginal benefits of actions exceed marginal costs. As they respond to opportunities, the system moves closer to equilibrium. The question is whether the opportunities they discover and the actions they take will increase wealth for society or simply redistribute existing wealth.

If entrepreneurs face the full opportunity costs of their actions, they will take only those actions that produce positive net benefits for themselves and for society. The entrepreneur who discovers a higher valued use for water, for example, stands to gain. If allocation to that higher use requires the entrepreneur to bear the opportunity costs of current use, the reallocation will only take place if the net difference is positive. Responsibility for opportunity costs is crucial.

As the rules of the game determine who has access to and use of resources, the property rights structure will determine who is responsible for which opportunity costs. If these rules are to govern market allocation of natural resources, property rights must be well-defined, enforced, and transferable. Well-defined property rights give individuals a clear idea of what actions they can take regarding resources—a necessary condition for market trades, which depend on interested parties knowing just what is being traded. Market allocations of water, for example, require that certain things be specified, such as units of measure and superiority of rights.

Enforcement determines how likely it is that an owner can enjoy the benefits of his ownership. Since rights cannot be perfectly enforced, ownership will always be probabilistic; but when the probability of capturing benefits from a use is low, it is less likely that the owner will devote the resource to that use. For example, if a water owner decides to leave water in the stream to improve fish habitat but is unable to exclude fishermen from using the stream, he will have less incentive to provide water for that use. In this sense, enforcement is the ability to exclude other users. As long as exclusion is possible, owners can capture the benefits from the uses of their resources.

Finally, property rights must be transferable if the owner is to be fully aware of the opportunity costs of his actions. When the owner is not allowed to transfer his resources to another use, he will not consider the full opportunity costs of that use. If the alternative use has a higher value, that value will be ignored and inefficiency will be the result. Laws forbidding the use of water in coal slurry pipelines, for example, tell water owners to ignore the value of water in this use. Even if water used for a coal slurry has more value than water used for irrigation, the owner cannot capture the higher value.

It is important to emphasize that all decisions are made under conditions of uncertainty and mistakes will be made. When an entrepreneur moves a resource from one use to another, he does so with the *expectation* that the new use has a higher value. This expectation depends on the entrepreneur's subjective evaluation of the world. The basic economic problem, therefore, becomes one of using "knowledge which is not given to anyone in totality."[12] As Friedrich Hayek has pointed out, the refinements in the neoclassical model have tended to divert attention from this problem, focusing instead on the possibility of planning. The realization that knowledge is dispersed and cannot be condensed into a single variable for planning purposes and that entre-

[12]Friedrich A. Hayek, "The Use of Knowledge in Society," *Individualism and Economic Order* (Chicago: Henry Regnery, 1972), p. 78.

preneurs make decisions based on their "best guess" about the future leads to the recognition that decisions may not be efficient *ex post.*

It is also important to remember that an optimal amount of search is involved. To the extent that entrepreneurs can gather information to reduce uncertainty, they will do so to the point where the expected additional benefits from the search activity equal the expected additional costs. Of course, what may be the optimal amount of search for one entrepreneur may not be optimal for another, so it is easy for observers to argue that better decisions could result if more information were collected. But perfect information is not the norm to which we should compare the real world.

What happens when private property rights do not exist and there is a gap between authority and responsibility? The entrepreneur continually searches for opportunities to generate returns above opportunity costs or rents. A system of efficient property rights will ensure that the entrepreneurial process will create rents, producing the only free lunch available to society. But the entrepreneur does not care whether he is creating a free lunch or dining at someone else's expense. Suppose the entrepreneur perceives two opportunities, one in which rents can be created through improved allocation of privately owned resources and one in which rents are derived from exploiting a common pool resource or from restricting entry.

First, consider the economics of a common pool resource and the inefficiency associated with a "tragedy of the commons."[13] Steven Cheung has shown how entrepreneurs, faced with a common pool resource, dissipate rents associated with private resource ownership.[14] For example, when an individual pumping from a groundwater basin observes others beginning to pump from the same source, he realizes that the water he leaves in the ground will be taken by the other pumpers. Therefore, he has an incentive to pump water until the net value of additional water is zero. Exploiting the common pool resource benefits the individual, but it is a negative-sum game for society.

Entrepreneurs also play a negative-sum game when they engage in rent seeking. Simply put, rent seeking occurs when decision-makers use the coercive power of government to increase personal wealth at the expense of others. For example, when a group of producers convinces the state legislature that all producers should be licensed, thereby

[13]Garrett Hardin, "The Tragedy of the Commons," *Science* 162 (1968): 1243–48.

[14]Steven N. S. Cheung, "The Structure of a Contract and the Theory of a Non-Exclusive Resource," *Journal of Law and Economics* 16 (1971): 49–70.

19

restricting entry, monopoly rents will be earned. Since these rents are earned at the expense of the consumer, they represent a redistribution of wealth. As a result, both producers and consumers will invest entrepreneurial talents and other resources in efforts to prevent or obtain the transfer. In many cases, for example, zoning restrictions and restrictions on water use represent a taking and redistribution of rights. When the Department of Interior decides whether public lands will be used for recreational or municipal uses, it affects the distribution of benefits and costs. The decision on whether to explore for oil in the Bob Marshall Wilderness Area in Montana determines whether environmentalists will continue to enjoy current amenity values or whether energy companies and consumers will have more energy reserves. Interest groups spend large amounts of money and other resources trying to influence these decisions. When the entrepreneur discovers opportunities to use government to increase his wealth through subsidies, barriers to entry, grants, and so on, rent creation—a positive-sum game—is replaced with rent seeking—a negative-sum game.

Such entrepreneurial efforts explain the demand for rent seeking; the activities of politicians and bureaucrats explain the supply. Just as entrepreneurs in the marketplace recognize and fill demands for goods and services, politicians and bureaucrats discover opportunities to meet the demands of their constituencies. The constraints on each, however, are very different. Private entrepreneurs provide new goods and services only if the benefits from those goods and services exceed the opportunity costs of the resources used in production. Politicians or bureaucrats who provide goods and services to interest groups do not have to pay the opportunity cost of expended resources.

Property rights to resources that are "owned" by the government are only informally defined and can be disputed at every legislative session. For example, the Bureau of Reclamation "owns" vast amounts of water. Rights to use this water are informally held by the groups who derive benefits from them. Since these rights are informal, if agricultural interests want an increase in irrigation withdrawals, they can attempt to convince bureaucrats to take rights away from recreation groups. If the bureaucrat does so, he might be concerned with alienating the recreation groups, but he does not have to face the full opportunity costs of his action.

In seeking to maximize budgetary discretion, each bureaucrat realizes that he has access to the common pool of the government treasury.[15]

---

[15]John Baden and Rodney Fort, "Natural Resources and Bureaucratic Predators," *Policy Review* 11 (Winter 1980): 69–82.

He asks, "What is the gain to my organization (and, hence, to me) of capturing another increment of the treasury?" The increase finances his agency's activities, and the costs of his capture are spread among all other bureaucracies in terms of lost capture opportunities. In order to increase his agency's capture, each bureaucrat must find ways to increase the magnitude and scope of agency activity, so he pursues programs that concentrate benefits and disperse costs. In this way, agencies build a constituency for increased activity.

Since opportunity costs are not internalized in the political allocation process, there is no direct reality check on whether a given situation can be improved, making it possible for enterprising politicians and bureaucrats to pursue inefficient policies. The economics of public choice teaches us to view public sector activities like any other activity. Politicians and bureaucrats are trying to maximize certain objectives, such as votes, budgets, power, prestige, and discretion. As these goals are pursued through collective action, public decision-makers face cost functions that differ from those where voluntary consent is required. Essentially, collective action allows those who bear the costs to be separated from those who receive the benefits.

Building on the premise that actors in the political system are likely to be motivated by self-interest, the public choice paradigm has uncovered several reasons why governmental action has failed to meet efficiency criteria:

1. *Voter ignorance and imperfect information.* In a democratic society, where it is unlikely that any voter, even a well-informed one, can influence the outcome of the political process, the benefits of being well-informed cannot be fully captured by the individual. At the same time, obtaining information about candidates and issues is costly for the voter. Thus, voters remain rationally ignorant; that is, they do not undergo great costs to obtain information except on issues that are important to them personally.

2. *Special interest effects.* Those voters who do become well-informed and politically active on any issue tend to be those who will benefit from a particular governmental action. With benefits concentrated on a few recipients, it is worth the recipient group's time to try to bring about specific governmental action. Since the costs of governmental action—subsidies, transfer payments, tariffs, regulations, etc.—tend to be diffused over the entire population of taxpayers and consumers, any action costs each individual so little that it is not worth his time to organize in opposition. With the combination of concentrated benefits and diffused costs, well-informed and articulate interest groups (which

contribute to campaigns) will dominate the political process and receive political favors.

3. *Shortsighted effects.* Politicians who must face the electorate every few years tend to be more concerned with the short run than with the long run. They will have little interest in policies that are efficient but that take time to produce results.

4. *Little incentive for candidates to account for individual preferences.* In the marketplace, consumers are generally able to tailor their purchases very closely to their own preferences, and each individual gets the particular kind of product he wants. In the political marketplace, however, voters must decide on alternative bundles of governmental expenditure and tax proposals offered by competing politicians. There is no opportunity for individuals to pick some of one candidate's positions and some of another's, and at the same time reject both candidates' positions on other issues. To capture as many votes as possible, the candidates' policy bundles tend to reflect a majority coalition, not the wishes of individual voters.

Given these characteristics of the political sector, the information and incentive structures are likely to generate governmental failure. Not only does inefficiency result, but entrepreneurial talents are expended by interest groups trying to influence decisions and by politicians and bureaucrats trying to fill niches. Without the reality check found in the private sector, the potential for negative-sum games is very real. The most obvious examples of governmental failure in water resource management include energy policies that promote coal gasification and other synfuels projects that require large quantities of water, construction of dams that cannot pass the cost-benefit test, and subsidized delivery of water.

Summary

The dispersion of knowledge in society forces a consideration of processes rather than end-states. The neoclassical model has always focused on efficiency conditions that constitute end-state criteria, criteria that become meaningless from a planning perspective. But

> the economic problem of society is . . . not merely a problem of how to allocate "given" resources—if "given" is taken to mean given to a single mind which deliberately solves the problems set by the "data." It is rather a problem of how to secure the best use of resources known to any of the members of society, for ends whose relative importance only these individuals know.[16]

[16]Hayek, pp. 77–78.

The refinements made on neoclassical models of resource allocation produce an "economic calculus" that lends itself to planning. The marginal revolution and its extension in economics leads to the conclusion that economic problems can be solved simply by equating at the margin. But the real question is: What are the relevant margins and what value will be placed on them? Since the dispersion of knowledge in society prevents any individual or group from answering this question, end-states cannot be known. "The problem is thus in no way solved if we can show that all the facts, *if* they were known to a single mind . . . would uniquely determine the solution; instead we must show how a solution is produced by the interaction of people each of whom possesses only partial knowledge."[17] Put simply, resource allocation and resource policy require an evaluation of process, a requirement met by the new resource economics paradigm.

The marginal conditions derived from complex, traditional models have little value for policy decisions. Not only do these models implicitly assume that knowledge is given, they assume that knowledge will be used by a dispassionate, highly organized, professional technician who will apply scientific principles to resource management. Traditional economic models seem to be based on the assumption that efficient resource allocation can be achieved by a few expert managers. But where do we find them?

The new resource economics takes a different approach, examining individual behavior with the assumption that self-interest prevails. If authority can be linked to responsibility through private property rights, self-interest can be linked to efficiency. In the absence of such a link, nothing in the economic process will push the system toward efficiency. Since it is probable that no one except economists cares about efficiency, it should not be surprising to find that marginal conditions have provided little guidance for policy decisions. This is not to say that marginal conditions are irrelevant, but we should focus more on the process and the constraints on individual actions that determine whether the marginal conditions are likely to be met.

How does the new resource economics paradigm fit into the mainstream of natural resource economics? Alan Randall, in one of the few natural resource economics texts, has argued that mainstream economists fall into several loose groupings:

> The middle group is occupied by those who find the mainstream economic methodology useful, and even quite powerful, but who

[17]Ibid., p. 91.

realize that it has some perplexing limitations, especially when applied to policy analysis. . . . To one side of the middle, there is a group of free-market zealots, who see the economic system in very simple terms, and who cannot understand why others fail to see what, to them, is obvious. They divide their time between proselytizing for free-market solutions among non-economists and attempting to keep the other groups of mainstream economists on the straight-and-narrow. To the other side of the middle, there is an ill-defined group of those who are quite uneasy about the limitations of mainstream economics in policy analysis, 'and suspicious that the zealots confuse methodology and ideology but are unable to develop a coherent alternative to the mainstream methodology.[18]

Although the approach taken in this book lies on the free-market side of the middle, this does not imply zealotry. Belief in the ability of the market system to coordinate resource allocation is derived from a preponderance of evidence supporting the efficiency that results when market processes are applied to water problems. The approach taken here will not offer much hope to the central water planner who wants to supplant entrepreneurial decisions with bureaucratic ones. The emphasis on decentralized decision processes that offer the potential for generating positive-sum games will, however, offer hope and encouragement to those who value efficiency, productivity, and individual freedom.

[18]Randall, p. 37.

III. The Evolution of Water Institutions

People produce the institutions, or rules of the game, that govern their behavior. Therefore, people will devote their efforts to defining and enforcing the rules as long as their perceived additional benefits from doing so exceed their perceived additional costs. In this sense, establishing and protecting property rights is a productive activity toward which resources can and will be devoted.

At any point in time, a unique amount of effort will be put into definition and enforcement activities, and that amount will be where the net return from effort is maximized. Just as there are diminishing returns to using more fertilizer on a field, there are diminishing returns to definition and enforcement activity. While the added benefits of producing property rights decline, the added costs rise. Following standard economic reasoning, resources used to produce property rights must be attracted from other, higher-valued alternatives, increasing the opportunity cost of producing property rights. The combination of diminishing returns and rising costs limits the amount of resources that will be devoted to property rights production.

While this tells us that there is an equilibrium level of definition and enforcement activity, the more important question is why the level varies over time and between areas. The answer depends on the parameters that cause benefits and costs to change. The benefits will depend on the value of the asset and the degree to which definition and enforcement activity ensures that the value will be captured by the owner. Any change in the price of a well-defined and enforced bundle of rights changes the return on resources devoted to producing property rights.

Higher market values or greater scarcity will spur individuals to strengthen their claims to resources. Witness, for example, how as our air, water, and scenic vistas have become more scarce, individuals or groups have attempted to better define their claims on these resources. Further, as the probability of losing an asset increases, there will usually be an increase in the productivity of property rights activity. An increase in the neighborhood crime rate means that locks, burglar alarms, and watchdogs will have higher benefits than before because each does more to ensure appropriation of value. The probability of loss is also affected by such variables as population density, cultural and ethical attitudes, and the institutional structure.

The cost of defining and enforcing property rights is a function of the quantity of resources necessary for a given amount of activity and the opportunity cost of those resources. Hence, anything that reduces the quantity of resources or lowers the opportunity cost will cause a shift in definition and enforcement costs. Changes in technology, in resource endowments, and in the scale of operation could cause such a shift. A perfect example is the introduction of barbed wire in the 1870s. To the homesteader whose land was invaded by cowboys and their herds, barbed wire defined his private property. It also allowed stockmen to control grazing, to rotate cattle on pastures, and to selectively breed their livestock.

The production of property rights does not depend on formal government. As Harold Demsetz wrote, "property rights arise when it becomes economic for those affected by externalities to internalize benefits and costs."[1] In no place was this more evident than on the American frontier. Since the early settlers arrived in the West before the legal machinery of state and federal government could be established, they found it necessary to generate their own rules. Without the power of coercion granted to government, those rules depended on voluntary agreements among the settlers. Wagon trains, cattlemen's associations, and mining camps all provide excellent examples of the evolution of social contracts.[2] To be sure, not all people had equal power in the bargaining process, and in some cases the six-gun introduced an element of coercion; but the image of the Wild West often ignores the role that contracts played in establishing property rights. The role of contracts is nowhere more evident than in the evolution of Western water rights.

Riparian Rights vs. Prior Appropriation

To the frontiersmen entering the Great Plains, it was clear that access to water had to be a prime factor in considering a location. Hence, initial settlement patterns can be traced to the river and stream bottoms. If an individual found that a stream location was already taken, he

[1]Harold Demsetz, "Toward a Theory of Property Rights," *American Economic Review* 57 (May 1967): 354.

[2]See Terry L. Anderson and P. J. Hill, "The Evolution of Property Rights: A Study of the American West," *Journal of Law and Economics* 18 (April 1975): 163–79; and John Umbeck, "The California Gold Rush: A Study of Emerging Property Rights," *Explorations in Economic History* 14 (1977): 197–226.

simply moved to another water supply. Under these circumstances, the right to use the water accrued to whoever owned the stream bank and had access to it by virtue of position.

It is not difficult to understand why such riparian water rights, whether implicit or explicit, were adopted by the frontiersmen. These rights found historical precedent in Eastern laws, which had been borrowed from English common law. Early judges and lawyers in the West were only familiar with Eastern law and were inclined to transfer it to the legal system.[3] In addition, land with adjacent water was abundant relative to the number of settlers; that is, water was not a relatively scarce factor. As long as these conditions held, rights that granted all riparian owners equal use of the flowing stream sufficed for resource allocation. The benefits of changing the existing institutions governing water were not sufficient remuneration for the time and effort required to initiate the change.

Two factors worked to change the benefits and costs of altering property rights over water. First, mining technology required that water be taken from the stream and moved to nonriparian locations. Since the riparian rules gave all owners the right to an undiminished quantity and quality of water, diversions for mining and irrigation were not feasible. Second, a great deal of nonriparian agricultural land could be made more productive if irrigation water could be moved to it.

Since the California mining camps were the first to feel major population pressure, it is not surprising that miners played an important role in the evolution of the prior appropriation doctrine.

> Following a tradition of collective action on the mining frontiers of other continents, the miners formed districts, embracing from one to several of the existing "camps" or "diggings" and promulgated regulations for marking and recording claims. The miners universally adopted the priority principle, which simply recognized the superior claims of the first-arrival. . . . The miners' codes defined the maximum size of claims, set limits on the number of claims a single individual might work, and established regulations designating certain actions—long absence, long diligence, and the like—as equivalent to the forfeiture of rights. A similar body of district rules regulated the use of water flowing on the public domain.[4]

The miners quickly realized that gold was not only found along

[3]Walter Prescott Webb, *The Great Plains* (New York: Grosset and Dunlap, 1931), p. 447.

[4]Charles W. McCurdy, "Stephen J. Field and Public Land Law Development in California, 1850–1866: A Case Study of Judicial Resource Allocation in Nineteenth-Century America," *Law and Society Review* 10 (Winter 1976): 236–37.

streambeds, where only a pan and shovel were needed to extract the precious mineral. When deposits were discovered several miles from water, it made economic sense to appropriate water from the streams. "It universally became one of the mining customs that the right to divert and use a specified quantity of water could be acquired by prior appropriation."[5] These customs had

> one principle embodied in them all, and on which rests the "Arid Region Doctrine" of the ownership and use of water, and that was the recognition of discovery, followed by prior appropriation, as the inception of the possessor's title, and development by working the claim as the condition of its retention.[6]

While there is no question that the original mining law was aimed at establishing private rights to water through appropriation, disputes over rights led to court cases, which in turn led to conflicts with the riparian doctrine of common law. Judges were torn between their training, which taught them that decisions ought to "conform, as nearly as possible, to the analogies of the common law," and the Western tradition, which held that law "ought to be based on the wants of the community and the peculiar conditions of things."[7] The tensions between the riparian and prior appropriation doctrines are reflected in the finding by some courts that appropriative principles were "impractical" and the finding by others that cases "must be decided by the fact of priority." The result was an interesting and eventually harmful mix of Eastern and Western law. Webb has captured the nature of the mix:

> The Easterner, with his background of forest and farm, could not always understand the man of the cattle kingdom. One went on foot, the other went on horseback; one carried his law in books, the other carried it strapped round his waist. One represented tradition, the other represented innovation; one responded to convention, the other responded to necessity and evolved his own conventions. Yet the man of the timber and the town made the law for the man of the plain; the plainsman, finding his law unsuited to his needs broke it and was called lawless.[8]

From Eastern law came such concepts as usufruct, beneficial use,

---

[5]Ibid., p. 254.

[6]Clesson S. Kinney, *Law of Irrigation and Water Rights and Arid Region Doctrine of Appropriations of Waters*, vol. 1 (San Francisco: Bender-Moss, 1912), p. 598.

[7]*Hoffman* v. *Stone*, 7 Cal. 46, 48 (1957).

[8]Webb, p. 206.

and reasonable use. From the Western mining camps and cattle ranges came absolute property, equal footing for uses, and transferable ownership rights. The riparian doctrine maintained an element of common property by continuing to support the view that riparian owners have co-equal rights in the water; that is, when water is put to new uses, existing riparian users may be required to cease current uses to make way for new ones. Since riparian rights are generally not transferable, the possibility of market allocation is further restricted.

The doctrine of appropriations, on the other hand, established ownership rights that were clearly defined, enforced, and transferable. Rights were absolute and not co-equal. As a result, markets were left to determine the value of water. The California courts asserted that "a comparison of the value of conflicting rights would be a novel mode of determining their legal superiority."[9] As McCurdy stated, "Anyone might take and use water flowing on the public domain for any beneficial use subject only to the rights of any prior appropriators."[10] The doctrine of appropriations gave no preference to riparian landowners, allowing all users an opportunity to compete for water and to develop far from streams. Appropriations were limited according to the means used for appropriating or the purpose of the appropriation.

In many cases, disputes arose and courts were called on to define rights. Cases were often complicated, but Judge Stephen J. Field of the California Supreme Court contended that "the courts do not . . . refuse the consideration of subjects, because of the complicated and embarassing character of the questions to which they give rise."[11] The Field court continually worked to define and enforce rights in order to promote efficient markets. Even pollution, which frequently occurred in the mining process, was handled by having polluters pay damages to those users who received lower quality water. The impact of the Field court decisions can be summarized as follows:

> By converting the possessory claims of so many trespassers into judicially-cognizable property rights, the California court effectively brought federal land-use policy into the realm of private, and, in some instances, constitutional law. . . . Moreover, the court also mobilized the still inchoate "public purpose" and due process doctrines to prohibit the miners' "primary assemblages," as well as the state legislature, from using the organized power of the community to divest the equitably-

[9]*Weaver* v. *Eureka Lake Co.*, 15 Cal. 271, 175 (1860).

[10]McCurdy, pp. 257–58.

[11]*Butte Canal and Ditch Co.* v. *Vaughan*, 11 Cal. 143, 152 (1858).

acquired claims of men who had evinced a growth inducing "incentive to improvement." . . . Field believed that only the courts were capable of resolving allocation problems so as to simultaneously protect property rights, release entrepreneurial energies, and provide all men with an equal opportunity to share the material fruits of a vigorously-expanding capitalist society.[12]

The law that evolved in the West reflected the greater relative scarcity of water in the region. As the settlers devoted more efforts to defining and enforcing property rights, a system of water law evolved, which (1) granted to the first appropriator an exclusive right to the water and granted water rights to later appropriators on the condition that prior rights were met; (2) permitted the diversion of water from the stream so that it could be used on nonriparian lands; (3) forced the appropriator of water to forfeit his right if the water was not used; and (4) allowed for the transfer and exchange of rights in water between individuals.

Private Water Development

While the doctrine of appropriation was evolving in the mining camps, private institutions were developing to capture and deliver the water to where it was needed. One usually thinks of large federal reclamation projects as the main impetus to Western irrigation, but private development dominated the frontier. The American Indians and the Spaniards were the first to irrigate the American West, followed by such groups as the Mormons, who had 16,000 acres of irrigated lands under cultivation by 1850, 263,500 acres by 1890, and 1,176,116 acres by 1940.[13]

Cooperative colonies also made significant contributions to early irrigation development in the West. The Greeley Colony in Colorado, founded in 1870 and named after Horace Greeley, brought 32,000 acres under irrigation and set the stage for irrigation development in Colorado. The Anaheim Colony in California also demonstrated that private savings could finance the construction of irrigation canals. The main group involved in the cooperative stayed in San Francisco to work in order to finance the venture while others worked on the colony to produce crops on 20-acre, privately owned parcels irrigated by communally owned canals.

The contributions of private reclamation projects should not be

[12]McCurdy, pp. 264–66.

[13]Alfred R. Golze, *Reclamation in the United States* (Caldwell, Idaho: The Caxton Printers, 1961), p. 6.

30

underestimated. By 1910, over 13 million acres of land in the West were irrigated by private ventures. Between 1900 and 1910, the number of irrigated acres grew by 86.4 percent, with private enterprise accounting for almost all of the increase (see table 3).[14] Even though public development greatly increased after the Reclamation Act of 1902, private development continued to provide a significant portion of new irrigation development.

Many different forms of business organization were used to develop Western irrigation. For the smaller projects, especially in the mining districts, individuals and partners had sufficient funds to undertake the necessary investments. The cooperative ventures of the Greeley and the Anaheim colonies also contributed significantly. In 1920, cooperative ventures, including incorporated, unincorporated, and irrigation districts, irrigated more acres than individuals and partnerships (see table 4).

According to Rodney Smith, the private irrigation companies or mutual corporations usually organized themselves around six rules:

1. The company issued shares of stock which were similar to any privately owned corporation.
2. Each share was treated equally with the total number of shares

Table 3

PRIVATE IRRIGATION DEVELOPMENT IN 17 WESTERN STATES, IN ACRES

Census	Total Irrigated Acreage	Furnished Government Water	Private Development
1890	3,631,381	—	3,631,381
1900	7,527,690	—	7,527,690
1902	8,875,090	—	8,875,090
1910	14,025,332	568,558	13,456,774
1920	18,592,888	2,388,199	16,204,769
1930	18,944,856	3,049,970	15,894,886
1940	20,395,043	3,800,239	16,594,804
1950	24,869,000	5,700,000	19,169,000

SOURCE: Alfred R. Golze, *Reclamation in the United States* (Caldwell, Idaho: The Caxton Printers, 1961), p. 14.

[14]Ibid., p. 13.

Table 4

AREA IRRIGATED IN 17 WESTERN STATES, BY TYPE OF ENTERPRISE

Item and Type of Enterprise	Primary Enterprises (acres)		
	1920	1930	1940
Individual and partnership	6,448,663	6,038,835	6,906,738
Cooperative, incorporated	6,569,690	6,271,334	5,706,606
Cooperative, unincorporated	—	—	907,242
Irrigation district	1,822,887	3,452,275	3,514,702
Reclamation district	—	—	59,052
Commercial	1,635,027	999,838	855,166
Bureau of Reclamation	1,254,569	1,485,028	1,824,004
Bureau of Indian Affairs	284,551	331,840	515,765
State	5,620	11,472	16,995
City and/or sewage	40,146	121,218	83,457
Other	531,735	233,016	5,316
TOTAL	18,592,888	18,944,856	20,395,043

SOURCE: Alfred R. Golze, *Reclamation in the United States* (Caldwell, Idaho: The Caxton Printers, 1961), p. 99.

equaling the capacity of the irrigation system. Available water in any given year was prorated according to stock ownership.

3. The shares of stock were transferable, with prices determined in the marketplace. In most cases, owners could rent any or all of their water rights.
4. The expenses incurred by the company for operation maintenance service and retirement of debt were also prorated according to stock ownership.
5. Stockholders' liability was not limited. The land of the stockholder could be used as a lien against any financial obligations of the mutual.
6. Private irrigation companies had the power to condemn land for right-of-way, provided they paid just compensation.[15]

These rules are especially significant, since they further contributed to the operation of private markets in the West. By using members'

[15]Rodney T. Smith, "The Economic Determinants and Consequences of Private and Public Ownership of Local Irrigation Facilities," in *Water Rights: Scarce Resource Allocation, Bureaucracy, and the Environment*, Terry L. Anderson, ed. (Cambridge, Mass.: Ballinger Press, 1983).

assets as collateral, mutuals could enter capital markets to obtain the investment funds necessary to develop irrigation projects. The transferability of stocks ensured that water could be moved to higher valued alternatives, further ensuring the success of the operation. These features, combined with the security of rights provided by the doctrine of appropriation, stimulated an effective marketplace. Writing in 1903, Elwood Mead concluded that investment with corporate capital in canals

> has been the leading factor in promoting agricultural growth of the Western two-fifths of the United States. It has been the agency through which millions of dollars have been raised and expended, thousands of miles of canals constructed, and hundreds of thousands of acres of land reclaimed. It has been the chief agency in replacing temporary wooden structures by massive headworks of steel and masonry, and, by the employment of the best engineering talent and the introduction of better methods of construction, has promoted the economy and success with which water is now distributed and used.[16]

In discussing the water deeds or water-right contracts of the Colorado ditch companies, Mead concluded that "if the water of streams is public property, the public should show the same business ability in disposing of its property as those to whom its control is transferred. Colorado can learn something about the management of the water of streams by studying how canal companies dispose of the water which they appropriate."[17]

Summary

During the last half of the 19th century, the foundation was laid for an effective water market. Following the doctrine of prior appropriation, water rights were defined and enforced and made transferable. In part, it was a sense of justice that led the early settlers to allocate water rights on the basis of "first in time, first in right." Out of this doctrine grew an efficient set of institutions that allowed individual actors in the marketplace to determine the best uses of water. Authority was linked to responsibility, giving water owners the incentive to seek out the highest and best uses of the resource. The scarcity of water increased the benefits of activities designed to establish and enforce exclusivity. Therefore, it is not surprising to find that in Montana, Wyoming, Colorado, and New Mexico, where rainfall averages 15

[16]Elwood Mead, *Irrigation Institutions* (New York: Macmillan Co., 1903), p. 57.
[17]Ibid., p. 167.

inches per year, the common law was eventually abrogated, while in North Dakota, South Dakota, Nebraska, Kansas, Oklahoma, and Texas, the common law was retained in a modified form. The evolution of water law on the Great Plains was a response to the benefits and costs of defining and enforcing rights to a valuable resource.

With an efficient set of water institutions in place, individuals undertook projects to deliver water where it was demanded. Well-defined exclusive rights provided the necessary tenure security to stimulate private investment. A variety of organizational structures were used to mobilize the necessary capital for building dams to store the water and aqueducts to deliver it. Irrigation and mining activities received most of the water, but population growth meant that municipal demands also had to be served. The leaders of the reclamation movement at the turn of the century were correct in asserting that without the application of water, lands west of the 100th meridian would not be very productive. They failed to recognize, however, how effectively private institutions and markets could serve this purpose. Thousands of miles of ditches were constructed and millions of acres blossomed as a result of entrepreneurial efforts to use water.

None of this should imply that water rights and markets are without defects. Resources had to be used to define and enforce water rights and to resolve disputes over those rights. Disputes continually arose over who was first in time and what quantities of water were claimed. Water markets operated in a region and time where information travelled slowly and risks were great. As a result, it was not easy to mobilize capital to invest in water development.

The American frontier was an experiment with the evolution of property rights. Since the actors in that experiment had to bear the consequences of their actions, they developed institutions that conserved the resources with which they worked. The economic returns available on the frontier were associated with natural resources, so the first generation of Westerners developed an institutional framework that promoted the efficient allocation of those resources. In this way, they were able to increase their wealth in spite of harsh conditions. The rules of the game on the frontier unleashed the productive potential of entrepreneurs and allowed for what James Willard Hurst has called "the release of energy."[18] Wealth in the West still depends on natural resources, but we seem to have lost sight of the importance of private property rights and the role of entrepreneurship.

[18]James Willard Hurst, *Laws and Conditions of Freedom in the Nineteenth-Century United States* (Madison: University of Wisconsin Press, 1964).

IV. What Went Wrong?

The system of water rights that evolved during the late 19th and early 20th centuries was by no means perfect. When return flows were claimed by downstream users, conflicts resulted when upstream users changed the amount or location of diversion, leaving less water to flow downstream. Capital markets were in their infancy, so some economical water projects were probably not funded. This also meant that once a delivery system was in place, the owner had some market power when competitive systems were not built. Third-party effects also existed on the frontier, where the first-in-time, first-in-right attitude often allowed pollution to foul downstream flows. Frontiersmen were experimenting with new institutional arrangements and could not possibly establish rights that took all contingencies into account.

Despite the imperfections in the system, they provided no good reason for the extent of governmental intervention that has occurred during the 20th century. The early development of water institutions took place outside the framework of formal government, since contracting formed the basis of water rights and markets. Eastern institutions and laws were often not suited to the resource endowments of the American West and had to be modified or abandoned. As formal courts and judicial procedures were established, lawyers brought with them the baggage of Eastern law and the formal powers of the federal government. As a result, it was not long before the institutions that evolved through spontaneous order were changed. Perhaps the Colorado mining district knew what it was doing when it resolved that "no lawyer be permitted to practice law in this district under penalty of not more than fifty nor less than twenty lashes, and be forever banished from the district."[1]

Rent Seeking Through Water Institutions

Economists define rent as the return from the employment of a resource that exceeds the opportunity costs of that resource. Rents,

---

[1]Quoted in J. H. Beadle, *Western Wilds and the Men Who Redeem Them* (Cincinnati, Ohio: Jones Brothers, 1882), p. 478.

therefore, provide a dynamic force to which entrepreneurs respond. It is rent that entrepreneurs try to capture when they move resources from lower- to higher-valued uses. When others observe these rents, they try to replicate the activity in an effort to capture a share. As long as property rights are well-defined and enforced, the only way an entrepreneur can do this is to improve resource allocation. In this sense, the entrepreneur provides the only free lunch available to society. As long as entry and exit from markets are possible, rents will signal opportunities for the efficient reallocation of resources. Such efforts to reallocate resources are known as productive or pie-enlarging activities.

Rents can also be obtained by using the coercive power of government to restrict entry or exit into a particular endeavor or to redistribute existing rights. Suppose, for example, that a firm's production activities generate water pollution. If the firm can persuade politicians to pass legislation that prohibits new firms from producing pollution, it will capture some rents. Similarly, if a special interest group successfully obtains subsidies for water development, there will be a redistribution of income and rents to those who receive the water.

Such efforts to influence governmental decisions are known as rent seeking. There is a possibility of rent seeking when the government can create barriers to entry and redistribute rights. Under these conditions, both losers and gainers will devote entrepreneurial talents to the political arena, where they will be used to influence decisions. Rent seeking then becomes a negative-sum game that reduces the size of the pie. As long as entrepreneurs believe that rents exist, competition among rent seekers will continue to dissipate the gains, using valuable resources in the process.

This country's Founding Fathers understood that self-interested individuals would attempt to use the government for rent seeking, so they erected constitutional barriers to prevent it.[2] During most of the 19th century, the contract clause, the commerce clause, and the due process amendments were all interpreted by the Supreme Court in ways that reduced the prospects for rent seeking. By prohibiting the government from interfering with contracts or exchange (commerce) and by ensuring that rules of law had to be followed, Court interpretations encouraged productive activity and generated substantial economic growth. During the last quarter of the century, however, the door was held

[2]See Terry Anderson and Peter J. Hill, *The Birth of a Transfer Society* (Stanford, Calif.: Hoover Institution Press, 1980).

open for rent seeking as more and more regulation of the marketplace was introduced.[3]

In light of constitutional barriers and fairly well-established water rights, how and why did rent seeking become institutionalized? The first justification used by legislatures and courts for governmental intervention in water institutions centered on the uniqueness of the resource. The ever-changing physical nature of water makes it difficult to define and enforce rights to it. As Blackstone said, "water is a moving, wandering thing, and must of necessity continue to be common by the law of nature; so that I can only have a temporary, transient, usufructuary property therein."[4] The second justification was provided by John Wesley Powell's 1878 survey of the Rocky Mountain region, which made people keenly aware of how important water really was in the arid West.

While it is true that water could make the desert bloom even as a rose and that it is a moving, wandering thing, it is not so unique that it requires the government to control its allocation. Water certainly is necessary for life, but clothing and shelter are also necessities, and there is no justification for their public allocation.

> This is not to deny that, as a commodity, water has its special features; for example, its supply is provided by nature partly as a store and partly as a flow, and it is available without cost in some locations but rather expensive to transport to others. Whatever reason we cite, however, the alleged unique *importance* of water disappears upon analysis.[5]

Nonetheless, it was this uniqueness that "led to the near-universal view that private ownership is unseemly or dangerous for a type of property so uniquely the common concern of all."[6]

Paraphrasing a section of the Water Rights Act of Iowa (substituting land for water), Jack Hirshleifer et al. have illustrated the absurdity of the uniqueness argument:

> *Land* occurring in any valley, or along any water course or around any other natural body of water in the state, is thereby declared to be public *land* and the public wealth of the people of the State of Iowa

---

[3]For a more detailed discussion, see ibid.

[4]Quoted in Walter Prescott Webb, *The Great Plains* (New York: Grosset and Dunlap, 1931), p. 434.

[5]Jack Hirshleifer, James C. DeHaven, and Jerome W. Milliman, *Water Supply: Economics, Technology, Policy* (Chicago: University of Chicago Press, 1960), pp. 4–5.

[6]Ibid., p. 367.

and subject to use in accordance with the provisions of this act, and the control and development and use of *land* for all beneficial purposes shall be in the state, which, in the exercise of its police powers, shall take such measures as shall perpetuate full utilization and protection of the *land* resources of the State of Iowa.[7]

Although most people would not accept this reasoning for the control of land resources, it has been used to further the public allocation of water.

Those who have argued for the government's involvement in water allocation have focused on three types of market failure: monopoly, imperfect capital markets, and externalities. Early water reformers feared that private water supplies would constitute a natural monopoly, which would allow suppliers to charge high prices for the resource. William Smythe stated the fear clearly:

> If we admit the theory that water flowing from the melting snows and gathered in lake and stream is a private commodity belonging to him who first appropriates it, regardless of the use for which he designs it, we have all the conditions for a hateful economic servitude. Next to bottling the air and sunshine no monopoly of natural resources would be fraught with more possibilities of abuse than the attempt to make merchandise of water in an arid land.[8]

Even though Powell recognized that the cheapest and most dependable source of water was from water companies selling at a profit, he was concerned with "the danger of an evil monopoly which would charge an exorbitant price and force the home steaders to pay a heavy tribute."[9] This concern contributed significantly to the government's growing involvement in the control of water rights and distribution.

The fear of monopoly, however, has little empirical basis. While it is true that water companies sold a product that was fairly inelastic in demand, many of those companies were not financially profitable, suggesting that their so-called monopoly power was not all that great. Companies did not compete with one another to provide irrigation water to the same regions. If one company raised its price too much trying to appropriate settlers' rents, the settlers could, without too much trouble, move to lands irrigated by cheaper water. As technology

[7]Ibid.

[8]Quoted in Richard Moss Alston, "Commercial Irrigation Enterprise: The Fear of Water Monopoly and the Genesis of Market Distortion," Ph.D. diss., Cornell University, 1970, p. 128.

[9]Quoted in ibid., p. 129.

was developed that allowed irrigation from groundwater sources, this possibility was even greater. Further, those commercial companies that were the only suppliers of water to a region had, for the most part, only one group of buyers. This situation led to possibilities for a bilateral monopoly, where irrigation companies and farmers bargained over the price of water. Just as water companies could attempt to appropriate rents to the land by raising prices, farmers could band together in attempts to expropriate rents to capital by forcing prices down. Finally, water companies could only effectively execute monopoly power if they could withhold their product from the market, an action requiring large storage facilities. Companies may have been able to hold back enough water to keep prices up temporarily, but eventually the water would have to be released, even from the largest facilities. When this water was released, the courts held that the water was free to be claimed by others. Therefore, the possibility of increasing prices by restricting output was unlikely.

Another reason given to support nonmarket alternatives to water allocation was that capital markets were unable to provide the investment funds necessary for large projects. Alfred Golze has stated that "while private enterprise had managed to bring under successful irrigation an impressive and substantial acreage of land, a point had been reached where further development would need stronger support by the Federal and state governments."[10] Even though water reformers recognized that capital markets had raised enough funds to build many irrigation projects, their visions encompassed such large-scale reclamation that no one could believe that private capital would be sufficient. In 1902, it was difficult to envision a world capital market that would be as extensive as it is today. Such a market did develop, however, and generates funds that could undertake many reclamation projects. An added deterrent to capital investments was the early support of many reclamation projects that simply could not pass the cost-benefit scrutiny of the marketplace. These projects would not have been profitable for private enterprise and were not profitable for the public either.

There was one more argument for governmental intervention in water allocation: The physical nature of water produced third-party effects, or externalities. If one user polluted a stream, the pollution moved downstream to affect other users. If one user pumped water from a common groundwater source, other users' pumping costs could

[10]Alfred R. Golze, *Reclamation in the United States* (Caldwell, Idaho: The Caxton Printers, 1961), p. 12.

be affected. In some cases, such concerns were warranted; the potential for externalities is one of the more powerful arguments economists use to justify nonmarket alternatives. The fact is, however, that the evolving system of water rights on the frontier was internalizing many of the external problems. In the case of pollution from mining operations, the courts "issued injunctions when debris buried the claims of miners below, destroyed the growing crops of preemption claimants, filled irrigation ditches and poisoned their fruit trees, or split the hoses of hydraulic miners downstream."[11] In *Jennison* v. *Kirk,* a California case in which a miner was held liable for damages when debris washed away the ditch of another appropriator, Judge Stephen Field ruled that "no system of law with which we are acquainted tolerates the use of one's property in that way so as to destroy the property of another."[12] Externalities do present real problems for markets, but they are overused as an argument for governmental intervention in water markets.

Rent seekers who used the coercive powers of government to obtain control of water rights or subsidies for irrigation projects made very successful use of these arguments. Backed by such public reclamation entrepreneurs as John Wesley Powell, Arthur P. Davis, and Elwood Mead, politicians saw an opportunity to provide their constituents with rents that could be created by restricting entry or by giving subsidies to special interests. Rent seekers claimed that

> federal control would promote "scientific" management of land and water resources, simultaneously "conserving" and "developing" them; prevent the monopolization of water by corporations and "speculators"; streamline the system for establishing and enforcing water rights; and encourage the development of rural democracy by war veterans and other deserving pioneers. These policies received the strong backing of at least three presidents including the two Roosevelts and Herbert Hoover.[13]

Limits on the Doctrine of Appropriations

The American West was evolving an effective system of water rights, provisions had been made for definition and enforcement, and rights

[11]Charles W. McCurdy, "Stephen J. Field and Public Land Law Development in California, 1850-1866: A Case Study of Judicial Resource Allocation in Nineteenth-Century America," *Law and Society Review* 10 (Winter 1976): 262.

[12]*Jennison* v. *Kirk,* 98 U.S. 453, 461 (1878).

[13]Alfred G. Cuzan, "Appropriators vs. Expropriators: The Political Economy of Water in the West," in *Water Rights: Scarce Resource Allocation, Bureaucracy, and the Environment,* Terry L. Anderson, ed. (Cambridge, Mass.: Ballinger Press, 1983).

were transferable. All the necessary ingredients existed for an effective water market to allocate the scarce resource. How did the transformation to centralized control take place?

The California court, under the direction of Judge Field, recognized the potential for "using the organized power of the community to divest the equitably-acquired claims of men who had evinced a growth inducing 'incentive to improvement.' "[14] But in the late 19th century, inefficient restrictions were placed on the doctrine of appropriations. State laws had come to recognize prior rights, but Western state constitutions and statutes were moving toward the establishment of the public ownership of water. Appropriators received only a usufructuary right (a right to use the water), not an actual ownership right, so state legislatures felt free to declare that the *corpus* of water was state property. Making this distinction contrasted sharply with existing land laws and created tension between use and ownership. As long as water was publicly owned, it was easy to exploit the potential for gain from regulation of its use.

As population and demands for water in the West grew, so did the number of disputes over ownership. When water was abundant, it did not pay to get involved in the disputes; but as the value of water rose, it became rational to devote resources to the fight. From the outset of the doctrine of appropriations, courts were involved in settling conflicting claims, with the costs being borne by those directly involved. But some found it profitable to have states subsidize this process. In 1874, for example, irrigators in Colorado "met in convention to demand legislation for public determination and establishment of rights of appropriation, and the state superintended distribution of water in accordance with the thus settled titles."[15] The transformation from prior appropriation to administrative law eventually brought with it

> requirements for the filing of new claims, first at the county, then the state level; the limitations on the size of "excessive" claims and legal specifications on the duty of water; attachment of water rights to specific land tracts; the disallowing of ownership to water by canal companies which did not irrigate lands of their own; regulation of canal company rates by states and counties; state encouragement to the formation of irrigation districts with the power to tax, condemn property and sell bonds to finance construction of irrigation works and buy out water companies; legislative determination of what con-

[14]McCurdy, p. 265.

[15]Moses Lasky, "From Prior Appropriation to Economic Distribution of Water by the State—Via Irrigation Administration," *Rocky Mountain Law Review* 1 (April 1929): 173.

stitutes "beneficial use," along with the ranking of uses by classes; prohibition on sale of water rights beyond state or irrigation district boundaries; administrative allocation of water during periods of "drought"; and the establishment of the centralized bureaucracy headed by a state engineer or water commissioner to administer policies and judicial decrees and, in some states, undertake irrigation projects.[16]

Judges also contributed to the erosion of the doctrine of prior appropriations by failing to abandon the common law precedent of riparian rights. Riparian rights grant that

> every owner of land through which a natural stream of water flows, has a usufruct in the stream, as it passes along, and has an equal right with those above and below him to the natural flow of the water in its accustomed channel, without unreasonable detention or diminution in quantity or quality, and to the reasonable use of the stream for every beneficial purpose to which it can be applied, and none can make any use of it prejudicial to the other owners, unless he has acquired a right to do so by license, grant or prescription.[17]

Some elements of the riparian doctrine led directly to more public control of water allocation. First, with riparian ownership the resource is held in common, requiring regulations on open access. Second, since uses that were prejudicial to other owners required "license, grant or prescription," users naturally sought and obtained these preferences through legislation.

Miners had presented the courts with a fairly well-settled doctrine for defining, enforcing, and transferring rights; but as disputes came before the courts, riparian arguments were continually introduced. As early as 1853, the California Supreme Court argued in *Eddy* v. *Simpson* that "the owner of land through which a stream flows, merely transmits the water over its surface, having the right to its reasonable use during its passage. The right is not in the corpus of the water, and only continues with its possession."[18] Though the ruling was subsequently overturned, a riparian precedent was established in California. Courts continued to hold that rights were only usufructuary and that they were lost once the water left the possession of its appropriator. John Clayberg saw how riparian principles were contributing to the evolution of the doctrine of appropriations:

[16]Cuzan, p. 13.

[17]*Heath* v. *Williams*, 43 Am. Dec. 265–275.

[18]*Eddy* v. *Simpson*, 3 Cal. 249, 252 (1853).

> There never seemed any doubt in the mind of the court about the true position to be taken, but it is almost amusing to read their statements as to whether the principle announced was in consonance with the common law, or in departure from it, because of the conditions and necessities of the case. In one case the court would say that they did not depart from the common law but found principles there insufficient to sustain their holdings. In another, the doctrine would be announced that the common law was inapplicable, and that the reasons of that law did not exist in California.[19]

The inability of lawyers and judges to put aside riparian precedent and the resultant mixture of riparian with prior appropriation doctrine led to a confusion that stifled the effective establishment of private property in water. Without private property rights, the confusion could only be resolved through legislation and administration.

The doctrine that had evolved through the spontaneous order and decentralized actions of miners and irrigators was slowly degenerating to the status of state-controlled permits and licenses. As early as 1929 Moses Lasky declared that the principle of appropriation had reached its zenith. The water rights that evolved in the quasi-anarchistic setting of the frontier were replaced by permits to use state-owned water, with decisions on water use ultimately determined by state officials. Lasky argued that these changes were causing a move *away* "from various forms of extreme individualism and vested property rights of substance in water to . . . the economic distribution of state-owned water by a state administrative machinery through state-oriented conditional privileges of user."[20]

The commerce clause of the Constitution also contributed to increased governmental regulation of water rights. Under the auspices of the commerce clause, the federal government chose to regulate all navigable waterways and their tributaries, effectively preventing private parties from developing reservoirs or rivers. The commerce clause had been interpreted as giving the government power to regulate interstate commerce, so the federal government used it to restrict water development on the grounds that it might impede navigation. With navigation defined in terms of the ability of streams to float logs, few streams were exempt from regulation. Charles Corker noted the implications of the power of the navigation doctrine:

[19]John B. Clayberg, "The Genesis and Development of the Law of Waters in the Far West," *Michigan Law Review* 1 (November 1902): 97–98.

[20]Lasky, p. 162.

> The Congress and the courts have been content to treat the word "navigation" as an open sesame to constitutionality. So long as Congress uses the word in statute and the case relates to something moist, the Court takes at face value the declaration that the legislation is in furtherance of navigation. Moreover, the tests of what constitutes a navigable stream has been stretched to embrace most of the waters of the United States. . . .[21]

The navigation doctrine continues to muddle water rights. In Montana, for example, a group is currently trying to secure public access to the Deerborn River, claiming that a rancher cannot prevent access because the stream is navigable. Even though the stream has not been used in recent years for floating logs, the issue centers on whether it *was* used for this purpose in the late 1800s.

By using legislative and administrative rules, individuals have been able to limit water rights in order to capture artificial rents. For example, using the argument that the doctrine of prior appropriations is "unfair," junior users have persuaded some state legislatures to substitute a different system of priorities than that provided in first-in-time, first-in-right. Preference is usually given to domestic and agricultural uses, with commercial and industrial uses having a lower priority. Therefore, even if commercial and industrial users purchase early water rights, those rights may be superseded. Similarly, legislation requiring forfeiture of rights for non-users has created the "use it or lose it" principle. While such laws were passed in an effort to prevent waste, they have created waste by encouraging water owners to use the water. The water owners are faced with a situation in which conservation could result in a loss of rights.

Perhaps the most obvious example of rent seeking exists in those states where allocative decisions are placed in the hands of the judiciary. When courts are asked to decide whether water should be used for agricultural or municipal purposes, for example, one group of individuals will lose and another will gain. The game is zero sum. Under these conditions, both groups will expend resources in the form of legal services to influence the judge's decision. In this way, a zero-sum game becomes a negative-sum game.

Rent seeking has also placed restrictions on the transferability of water rights. Frank Trelease has argued that such restrictions had their roots in the "many early adjudications that gave the irrigators far more

[21]Charles E. Corker, "Water Rights and Federalism: The Western Water Rights Settlement Bill of 1957," *California Law Review* 45 (1957): 616–17.

water than they really needed, so that the appropriator not infrequently sold his unused water to which he really had no right."[22] Through restrictions on transferability, some water users were able to gain by obtaining those "excessive" water rights. Hirshleifer et al. have observed that "an attempt to correct past mistakes in vesting property rights by simple deprivation or confiscation may have only distributional effects (except insofar as insecurity of rights affects incentive of others) but freezing the right to the original use of water has an adverse efficiency effect from which the community as a whole loses."[23] In Montana, for example, the state constitution prohibits the transfer and sale of water for use in coal slurry pipelines, suggesting that the state's constitutional reformers somehow knew that coal slurry would never provide a highest and best use for water. To the extent that restricted uses can compete with other uses, however, such provisions keep the price of water artificially low, providing a gain to some users at the expense of others.

Legal restrictions have essentially broken apart the foundation for an effective system of water rights that was built in the "lawless West."

> It is evident that the long-term trend of federal policy has been to mobilize financial, administrative, political, constitutional and judicial resources . . . to gain . . . control of western waters. . . . The appropriation doctrine has been undermined, water rights have been virtually expropriated and converted into licenses or permits, and control over Western waters has been centralized in state and federal governments.[24]

Instead of relying on markets, we have turned water allocation over to a rent-seeking process that uses valuable resources without guaranteeing efficiency or equity. If we are to avoid a water crisis through a market solution, we must return to the original principles of the appropriation doctrine.

Reclaiming the West with Public Funds

Just as limits on the appropriation doctrine hinder water markets, public reclamation replaced much private enterprise and created a bureaucratic pork barrel that continues to thrive even when other public funds are cut. What was the rationale for public investment in reclamation? How did it come about? What are its consequences?

In his *Report on the Lands of the Arrid Region* in 1878, Powell expressed

---

[22]Quoted in Hirshleifer et al., p. 235.

[23]Ibid., p. 24.

[24]Cuzan, pp. 20–21.

concern that water rights would be "gradually absorbed by a few. Monopolies of water will be secured, and the whole agriculture of the country will be tributary thereto—a condition of affairs which an American citizen having in view the interest of the largest number of people cannot contemplate with favor."[25] This concern, coupled with the argument that markets were not efficient enough to fund reclamation projects, led bureaucratic entrepreneurs to seek public funds for their large-scale plans to reclaim the American West.

Two pieces of legislation provided the cornerstone for governmental involvement in reclamation. First, the Wright Act was passed in California in 1887, providing the statutory emphasis for public ownership of irrigation facilities. The act also established a procedure for petitioning for and voting on the question of public control of irrigation. If half of the landowners holding 50 percent of the affected land petitioned for a public irrigation district, county commissioners were directed to call a special election in which a two-thirds majority was needed to establish the district. Once established, the irrigation district's board of directors could incur financial obligations, impose property taxes, and establish water prices. Even though these policies had to be approved by a majority of the voters, they paved the way for collective action to influence the distribution of benefits and costs of irrigation projects. Other Western states adopted similar legislation during the next few decades, and the door was open for rent seeking through irrigation districts. Unlike private, mutual companies, public irrigation districts could use property taxes to finance projects, creating the potential for income redistribution. Further, because neither the board of directors nor individual water users were residual claimants, the incentive for efficient pricing was greatly reduced. Irrigators who could keep the price of water below its opportunity cost received a rent or subsidy paid for by water district taxes.

Between 1920 and 1950, public irrigation districts in California grew from 577,000 irrigated acres to 1,821,000 irrigated acres. During this time, the number of mutual irrigation companies and commercial enterprises declined.[26] District organization reached its peak in the 1920s, while gross acreages of active districts remained fairly constant

[25]John Wesley Powell, *Report on the Lands of the Arrid Region of the United States*, 45th Cong., 2d sess., House of Representatives Ex. Doc. 73 (Washington, D.C.: Government Printing Office, 1878), p. 43.

[26]Rodney T. Smith, "The Economic Determinants and Consequences of Private and Public Ownership of Local Irrigation Facilities," in *Water Rights*.

until 1910, grew dramatically until 1925, and stabilized thereafter (see figure 1).

Rodney Smith's empirical analysis of the choice between private and public irrigation ownership in California supports the hypothesis that public districts provided a means for obtaining rents.[27] Mutual water companies charged direct prices, and public irrigation districts collected taxes, forming an implicit price. In mutual water companies, when individual water use increases, payments to the company increase. In public irrigation districts, however, an increase in an individual's water use influences not only his own property tax liabilities but also the liabilities of all other landowners in the district. Therefore, a farmer in a public irrigation district receives a direct benefit, and the costs are diffused over the district population. Smith demonstrated that water demand in mutual water companies is much more responsive to direct charges than water demand in public irrigation districts is to indirect taxes.[28] Pricing via taxes allows individuals to use public irrigation districts to redistribute income. Further, it promotes inefficient water use by allowing the irrigator to pay prices that do not reflect costs.

The Wright Act provided a local mechanism for subsidizing water projects. The Newlands Reclamation Act of 1902 took the process one step further by allowing the federal government to enter the water reclamation business in the West. Initially, reclamation projects were to be funded from the proceeds of public land sales. Costs were to be repaid within 10 years, though no interest charges were to be levied. Each Western state was to receive reclamation revenues according to its proportional contribution to the sales. By limiting water delivery to farms of 160 acres or less, the act was supposedly promoting Jeffersonian democracy, making rights to the water appurtenant to the land.

These initial provisions were relatively harmless in terms of subsidies to water users. The program was to pay for itself, but some were skeptical about the act from the beginning.

> A New York Congressman estimated that the plan would ultimately cost the country billions of dollars. Dalzell of Pennsylvania believed it a plan to "unlock the doors of the treasury." Mr. Cannon of Illinois dubbed the bill a "direct grant in an indirect way." Payne of New York was of a like mind, while Hepburn of Iowa insisted "that this is a thinly veneered and thinly disguised attempt to make the govern-

[27]Ibid.
[28]Ibid.

47

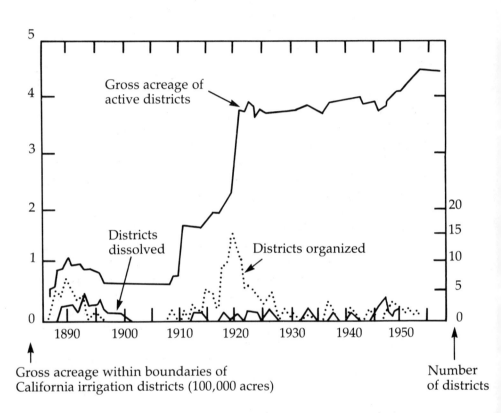

SOURCE: Michael F. Brewer, *Water Pricing and Allocation with Particular Reference to California Irrigation Districts* (Berkeley: California Agricultural Experiment Station, Giannini Foundation, 1960), figure 5.

48

ment, from its general fund, pay for this great work—great in extent, great in expenditure, but not great in results. . . ."[29]

In retrospect, the critics were right. The Reclamation Act has allowed irrigators and agents of the bureaucracy to engage in rent seeking. The projects allowed interest-free loans for construction costs, with flexible repayment schemes. By altering the terms of repayment, the Bureau of Reclamation was able to expand in size while irrigators were able to receive larger subsidies. The Reclamation Act also promoted rent seeking by setting the 160-acre limit. Since enforcement of the limit determined the distribution of benefits from federal irrigation programs, irrigators have attempted to alter the enforcement.

Though the initial legislation provided for 10-year, interest-free loans, the value of the subsidy to irrigators was increased significantly through extensions of the repayment period, allowances for periods with no repayment, and combinations of irrigation and power projects that allowed revenues from hydroelectric power to repay irrigation costs that exceeded the irrigators' "ability to pay." Table 5 shows the proportion of costs that were subsidized, depending on the interest rate and the repayment terms. The value of the subsidy was greatly increased by higher interest rates, longer repayment schedules, and grace periods. Because many Bureau of Reclamation projects were not economically sound, default was common. When loans could not be repaid, both farmers and bureaucrats argued for extensions, the graduation of payments, and the postponement of the date of first payment. The Omnibus Adjustment Act of 1926 compounded the problems by extending the prepayment of contracts to 40 years and by graduating the repayment schedule. When low agricultural prices between 1926 and 1930 made it difficult for farmers to meet their payments, Congress granted a moratorium on all payments from 1931 to 1936.

The Reclamation Project Act of 1939 empowered the Bureau of Reclamation to enter into even more flexible repayment contracts:

> Contracts negotiated under section 9(d) of this act were permitted to have repayment periods of 40 years with development periods of up to 10 years. The contracts could be written to allow for charges that varied with productivity of different classes of land within the project area and for annual changes that depended on gross crop values.[30]

[29]Benjamin H. Hibbard, *A History of the Public Land Policies* (Madison: University of Wisconsin Press, 1965), p. 442.

[30]Randall R. Rucker and Price V. Fishback, "The Federal Reclamation Program: An Analysis of Rent-Seeking Behavior," in *Water Rights*.

Table 5

THE INTEREST SUBSIDY

Payment Plan	Rate of Discount		
	3%	6%	10%
	Subsidized Proportion of Costs		
10-year repayment period; equal installments	14.7	26.4	38.6
20-year repayment period; equal installments	25.5	42.5	57.5
20-year repayment period; graduated installments*	28.9	47.8	64.0
20-year repayment period; graduated installments with grace period and down payment**	30.7	50.3	66.7
40-year repayment period; equal installments	42.3	62.5	75.5
40-year repayment period; equal installments with 10-year grace period	57.0	79.0	91.0

SOURCE: Randall R. Rucker and Price V. Fishback, "The Federal Reclamation Program: An Analysis of Rent-Seeking Behavior," in *Water Rights: Scarce Resource Allocation, Bureaucracy, and the Environment,* Terry L. Anderson, ed. (Cambridge, Mass: Ballinger Press, 1983).

*Repayment schedule (outlined in the act of August 13, 1914) was 2 percent of construction costs for first four years, 4 percent for next two years, and 6 percent for final 14 years.

**Repayment schedule (outlined in the act of August 13, 1914) was 5 percent of construction cost down, followed by a five-year development period, then annual payments of 5 percent for five years and 7 percent for the final 10 years.

In addition to giving irrigators larger subsidies, the ability to lengthen the repayment period gave the Bureau of Reclamation more long-term administrative control of projects, since control was not relinquished until a certain percentage of construction costs had been paid.

In the 1920s, the Department of Agriculture opposed Bureau of Reclamation irrigation projects on the grounds that they were aggravating the over-supply of farm products. In response, the Bureau became involved in multipurpose projects, building Hoover and Grand Coulee dams to provide hydroelectric power, municipal water, flood control, improved river navigation, and irrigation. Diversification gave the bureau support from other constituencies and enabled a further subsidization of irrigation water (see table 6). Subsidies to irrigation were running as high as 90 percent.

Summary

Between court cases and public reclamation efforts, there is little room left for the market allocation of water. In most Western states,

Table 6

THE POWER SUBSIDY

Project	Costs Allocated to Irrigation	Costs to be Prepaid by Irrigators	% of Irrigation Costs Subsidized
Central Valley California	682,152,000	606,646,000	11.1
Chief Joseph Dam Washington*	11,083,200	6,050,000	45.4
Collbran Colorado	6,105,000	1,089,101	82.2
Columbia Basin Washington	745,111,398	135,916,400	81.8
Fryingpan-Arkansas Colorado	69,946,000	50,512,300	27.8
Rouge River Oregon	18,064,000	9,066,500	49.8
San Angelo Texas	8,853,904	4,000,000	54.8
The Dalles Oregon	5,994,000	2,550,000	57.5
Ventura River California	18,273,128	10,746,300	41.2
Washita Basin Oklahoma**	10,403,011	8,221,000	21.0

SOURCE: See table 5.

NOTE: On some of these projects, a portion of the subsidy to irrigators came from industrial and municipal users. See Department of Interior, Bureau of Reclamation, *Reclamation Payments and Payout Schedule* (Washington, D.C.: Government Printing Office, 1965).

*Includes costs and repayments from Foster Creek and Greater Wenatchee divisions.
**Includes costs and payments from Fort Cobb and Fass divisions.

water is the declared property of the state, the people, or the public. Only in Colorado and New Mexico is this declaration limited to unappropriated water. Writing 20 years ago, Hirshleifer et al. concluded that

> the current trend . . . runs strongly against the development of a system of water law based on individual choice and the market mechanism. . . . the evidence is fairly clear that the tenor of the legislative and judicial edicts . . . is the product of the ignorance of even importantly placed and generally well-informed individuals today about the functioning of economic systems—and, in particular, it is the product of the common though incorrect opinion that the public interest can be served only by political as opposed to market allocation processes. . . . That there are defects in the present systems of private water rights is very clear; but to abolish property rights rather than cure the defects is a drastic and, we believe, unwise remedy.[31]

With few exceptions, legislative and judicial actions have continued to erode the basis of private property rights in water. Lasky's concern in 1929 over the shift from prior appropriation to economic distribution of water by the state was certainly prophetic.[32]

Large-scale federal involvement in reclamation has contributed to the demise of water markets and the promotion of inefficiency. Without proper information and incentives—that is, without residual claimants—alternatives to large-scale reclamation have not been considered carefully. For example, Rudolph Ulrich estimated that the costs of bringing desert land into agricultural production were 5 to 14 times greater than the costs of clearing, fertilizing, and irrigating lands in the humid Southeast.[33] In 1924, Benjamin Hibbard concluded that

> in passing the Reclamation Act in 1902 as a nation we clearly forgot those things which were behind, the millions of unoccupied acres of the Mississippi Valley, consisting mostly of fertile, well-watered land needing only to be drained or cleared. Had we really been concerned over the future food supply as we pretended to be, or being so concerned, had we calmly asked how to increase it in the cheapest and easiest manner, certain of the reclamation projects would still be undeveloped. . . .[34]

Reclamation may have made the desert bloom, but there is little economic justification for the blossoms.

[31]Hirshleifer et al., p. 249.

[32]Lasky, pp. 161–216.

[33]Randolph Ulrich, "Relative Costs and Benefits of Land Reclamation in the Humid Southeast and the Semi-arid West," *Journal of Farm Economics* 30 (1953): 62–73.

[34]Hibbard, p. 449.

V. Salvaging the Appropriations Doctrine

From the Western frontier, especially the mining camps, came the doctrine of appropriations and the foundation for a market in water. The Arid Region Doctrine, which governed the ownership and use of water, was based on "the recognition of discovery, followed by prior appropriation, as the inception of a possessor's title, and the development by working the claim as the condition of its retention."[1] This system provided the essential ingredients for an efficient market in water wherein property rights were well-defined, enforced, and transferable. With the rights to water clearly assigned, the owner was forced to bear the cost and was able to reap the benefits of his decisions. Mistakes were undoubtedly made, but water-rights owners had an incentive to learn from their mistakes and improve on water allocation in the process.

As the demand for water grew, so did the likelihood that some costs and benefits would not accrue to the individual decision-makers. Changes in water allocation by upstream users affected downstream users, and discharge of effluent into streams changed the quality of water for downstream recipients. Because of these third-party effects, legislatures, courts, and administrative agencies intervened in the market process by placing limits on water rights and on the ability of owners to transfer them. Since then, arguments alleging market failure and the recognition by special interest groups that government can be used to redistribute wealth have made the governmental allocation of water an acceptable policy.

Can the doctrine of appropriations be salvaged? Is there a legitimate rationale for restricting the transferability of water rights? Can third-party effects be resolved through alternative property rights, or must there be legislative, judicial, and administrative rulings? This chapter focuses on these questions.

---

[1]Clesson Kinney, *Law of Irrigation and Water Rights and Arid Region Doctrine of Appropriation of Waters*, vol. 1 (San Francisco: Bender-Moss, 1912), p. 598.

Alleged Market Failure

Traditional natural resource economists have approached the allocation of water resources from a market failure perspective, generally accepting the idea that externalities dominate water resource allocation and that legal restrictions on water transfers are necessary.

> In the natural resources field generally, the problem of externalities is widespread, and various organizational arrangements and regulatory measures have been adopted or proposed to cope with it. Laws have been written and established by courts to protect the third parties in water transfers. Special districts have been formed to internalize some of the externalities. The general tendency in institutional development has been to modify market procedures or completely replace them.[2]

Allen Kneese, director of the water resources program at Resources for the Future, has examined market failure in water allocation, claiming that there was a growing conceptual and research basis for devising more efficient water transfer mechanisms. Nevertheless, he concluded:

> It is not clear that the best means will be the exchange of water rights in markets because of the difficulty of arriving at reasonably certain definitions of rights when major third party effects, resulting from water quality deterioration and return flow dependency, are involved. Perhaps the most satisfactory solution will be some mixture of market transfers of rights and administrative allocations.[3]

Most recently, Charles Howe, Paul Alexander, and Raphael Moses argued that "if more than two users are involved, . . . any transaction between two users would ignore the return flow effects on the others."[4] Because of these inescapable externalities, they called for institutional reforms that utilize non-market allocation. First, they claimed, a more flexible water ownership system would establish "an agency that files for (or buys) water rights under state laws and sells the water produced to another entity. . . ."[5] Second, there should be an increased reliance on conservancy districts. Third, a state or interstate agency should be established to "make a market" in water rights: "Such an agency would

[2]L. M. Hartman and Don Seastone, *Water Transfers: Economic Efficiency and Alternative Institutions* (Baltimore: Johns Hopkins University Press, 1970), pp. 2–3.

[3]Allen E. Kneese, "Economic Related Problems in Contemporary Water Resource Management," *Natural Resources Journal* 5 (October 1965): 240.

[4]Charles W. Howe, Paul K. Alexander, and Raphael J. Moses, "The Performance of Appropriative Water Systems in the Western United States During Drought," *Natural Resources Journal* 22 (April 1982): 383.

[5]Ibid., p. 386.

stand ready to buy rights at a known schedule of prices and to sell rights to new users."[6] Fourth, better climatological data and forecasting programs would improve regional water programming. Finally, more training of water users, especially irrigators, would lead to a more efficient application of water. These proposals suggest that the market process can be replaced with planners using "known" schedules of demand and supply, but such institutional reforms ignore the important role of information and incentives provided by the market.

The conclusion that market failure is pervasive in water markets is certainly nothing new. Since the late 19th and early 20th centuries, there have been concerns about monopoly, imperfect capital markets, and third-party effects. Demands for governmental intervention have not been limited to water allocation, but such concerns did lead to some unique restrictions on water use, restrictions that have taken their toll on the market allocation process.

Frank Trelease has suggested that the objections to using the proven system of prior appropriations fall into two categories. The first centers on observed examples of apparent market failure, such as excessive water use, duplicating ditches, dry streambeds, and erosion. In many of these examples, however, market failure is not responsible; it is, rather, the fault of resource owners placing different, subjective values on the resource. "The mistake in these cases is the assumption that because these examples of defects can be found the defects are inherent in the system. Most of these distortions and dislocations . . . could be corrected by small adjustment of the system or tighter administration of the law."[7]

The second category of objections is based on theory. Trelease listed three "recurrent reactions":

> 1. A dislike of the "property system": Appropriators seize valuable interests in the public domain and enrich themselves at the expense of the public.
> 2. A mistrust of the "market system": A fear that under prior appropriation, water rights will become "frozen in the pioneer patterns," unsuitable for modern times and problems, and not just to reallocation to new uses and needs.
> 3. A dislike of the "priority system": In a shortage an "all-or-nothing" rule gives one of two essentially similarly situated water users all of his water while his neighbor gets none.

[6]Ibid., p. 388.

[7]Frank J. Trelease, "Alternatives to Appropriation Law," in *Water Needs*, Jed P. Nanada, ed. (Boulder, Colo: Westview Press, 1977), p. 60.

To a large extent these objections are based on lack of understanding—a failure to appreciate the flexibility and variety of operational methods available under controlled appropriation laws.[8]

The many objections to a laissez-faire water market resulted in restrictions on the property rights of water owners and the reduced efficiency of water markets. The restrictions fall into four basic categories: (1) beneficial use, (2) preferential use, (3) return flow, and (4) federal reclamation water use.

Beneficial Use

Beneficial-use restrictions are perhaps the oldest in the system of water rights, dating back to English common law. These restrictions found their way into the early mining camps where appropriators of water were required to put that water to beneficial use or lose it to other potential users. An 1897 Nevada court ruling in *Union Mill and Mining Co.* v. *Dangberg* was typical of early decisions that "under the principles of prior appropriation, the law is well settled that the right to water flowing in the public streams may be acquired by an actual appropriation of water for a beneficial use."[9] In the early mining camps, the beneficial-use requirement was established because it provided the most efficient way of enforcing property rights. While some inefficiencies undoubtedly resulted, beneficial use did make sense. Today, however, the "use it or lose it" principle has been codified in many states and encourages the wasteful application of water. When rights are well-defined, enforced, and tradable, there is little need for the state to intervene, since markets will ensure that water will be used for beneficial purposes. In many cases, the market may even encourage the conservation of water.

Beneficial-use restrictions also encourage individuals to use the law to preclude competing uses. If the state is to enforce the restrictions, it must specify what beneficial uses are. Water for domestic and agricultural purposes is seldom, if ever, excluded; but some states do not consider instream flows to fall into the category of beneficial use. For example, the Colorado Supreme Court ruled in 1965 that there was "no support in the law of this state for the proposition that a minimum flow of water may be appropriated in a natural stream for piscatorial purposes without diversion of any portion of the water 'appropriated' from

[8]Ibid.

[9]Quoted in Timothy D. Tregarthen, "The Market for Property Rights in Water," in *Water Needs*, p. 144.

the natural course of the stream."[10] In some cases, beneficial use is specified in the state constitution, as in Montana, where water cannot be used in coal slurry pipelines.

Beneficial-use restrictions allow competitors to keep the price of water artificially low by restricting competition. If those who want to use water for coal slurry were willing to pay $100 per acre foot and potential irrigators were willing to pay only $50 per acre foot, irrigators might favor precluding coal slurry as a beneficial use. "The doctrine of beneficial use, with its implications of judicial determination of need and non-use in effect increases the uncertainty of title to rights in water, and therefore reduces their marketability."[11] As long as beneficial use is determined in legislative, judicial, and administrative forums, a great deal of time, effort, and money will be devoted to the governmental process.

Preferential Use

Preferential-use restrictions have had similar consequences. Early rulings by the California Supreme Court "asserted that 'a comparison of the value of conflicting [water] rights would be a novel mode of determining their legal superiority.' Thus, it became a fundamental axiom that each of the purposes 'to which water is applied . . . stands on the same footing.' "[12] In 1876, the Colorado State Constitution declared that when water is used for the same purpose, priority and time shall determine the superior right; but "when the waters of a stream are not sufficient for all desiring its use, domestic use should have preference over agriculture and agriculture over manufacturing."[13] Most Western states have followed Colorado's precedent by including preferential-use restrictions in their constitutions or legal codes. Although there is a wide variation in preferences,

> there is general agreement only in that man's personal needs come first, so that domestic and municipal purposes head every list, and there seems to be fairly uniform resolve not to let waters run unused into the seas, with the consequence that power navigation operations are generally found near the bottom. But irrigation, manufacturing,

[10]*Colorado River Water Conservation District* v. *Rocky Mountain Power Company*, 158 Colo. 331, 406 P.2d 798, 800 (1965).

[11]Tregarthen, p. 145.

[12]Charles W. McCurdy, "Stephen J. Field and Public Land Law Development in California, 1850–1866: A Case Study of Judicial Resource Allocation in Nineteenth-Century America," *Law and Society Review* 10 (Winter 1976): 257.

[13]Trelease, "Preferences to the Use of Utility," *Rocky Mountain Law Review* 27 (1955): 134.

mining and railroad transportation jockey with each other for prefer-
ment in the middle ground.[14]

Because of preferential-use restrictions, some users have been given
the power to condemn so-called inferior rights. If a water owner values
his water more highly than does a competitor, the market would ensure
that he would not sell and that the water would remain in its highest
valued use. With preferential-use restrictions and the power to condemn, however, competitors can obtain the water provided they pay
"just compensation." Without the mutual consent of markets, compensation will be determined by the judicial process where opportunity
costs may be ignored. Many states give eminent domain powers

> to any person desiring to acquire the right to use water for a beneficial
> purpose, or provide for the condemnation of "inferior" uses in favor
> of "superior" ones, or that all water rights be condemned as the public
> interest and economy require. Little used to date, these statutes may
> provide a future need of readjusting water uses when maximum
> development has been reached, if the pattern of that development is
> not making the maximum contribution to the public welfare.[15]

Since 1955, competition for water, especially for municipal and instream
uses, has increased, and condemnation has become more common.
Preferential-use restrictions have worked hand-in-hand with beneficial-
use restrictions to reduce the security of water rights and encourage
rent seeking. The restrictions have been justified in the name of market
failure, but they have worked to weaken water rights established under
the doctrine of prior appropriation, thereby ensuring that markets will
not encourage efficient water allocation.

Return Flow

When water is diverted by an upstream user, some of the water is
returned either directly or indirectly to the stream to be claimed by a
downstream user. Some have argued that if the upstream user were to
change the point of diversion or the type of use, the return flow would
be altered and third-party impairment would result. The possibility of
third-party impairment has prompted many people to call for state
restrictions on transfers. In the Western states, either judicial or administrative procedures must be followed before water use or diversion
can be changed. In California, Idaho, Kansas, Nebraska, Mexico, Ore-

[14]Ibid., p. 158.
[15]Ibid., p. 138.

gon, Utah, Texas, and Washington, administrative agencies are empowered by law to approve or disapprove changes. In Arizona, Colorado, Montana, Nevada, North Dakota, and South Dakota, the judicial framework is used to determine whether changes in use or diversion should be allowed.[16]

Where administrative procedures are followed, if the owner of a water right wants to change the point of diversion or the method or place of use, he must petition the state water engineer. The state engineer is then charged with studying the proposal to determine whether third-party effects are involved. Usually the proposed change must be published in a regional newspaper, giving notice to other users of the stream system. If necessary, the state engineer may call for formal or informal hearings so that all evidence may be heard. Once a decision has been made, dissenters who believe that the change will be detrimental to the existing structure of rights can file suit in the appropriate court in an attempt to reverse the state engineer's decision. New Mexico state law is representative:

> An appropriator, with the approval of the State Engineer, may use water for a purpose other than for the purpose for which the water was appropriated, or may change the place of diversion, storage, or use, provided that no change may be allowed to the detriment of holders of valid and existing rights on the stream.[17]

The state engineer is empowered to

> make hydrographic surveys preparatory to adjudication of undecreed waters, to conduct studies to obtain basic hydrological data, and to make studies of water supply and water use. Other official functions are as follows: . . . to formulate plans for the orderly development of water resources of the State; and . . . to coordinate the work of various Federal, State, and local agencies in relation to programs of water development, conservation and use.[18]

In those states where transfers are adjudicated through the courts, the party seeking the transfer must file suit in the appropriate district court. "The purpose of this litigation is to allow the court to hear all protests to the transfer so that no person with alleged property rights in the water will be injuriously affected by the transfer."[19] The court

[16]Hartman and Seastone, *Water Transfers*, p. 16.

[17]New Mexico Statutes, Ann., 1953, sec. 75-5-23.

[18]Quoted in Hartman and Seastone, *Water Transfers*, p. 20.

[19]Ibid., p. 19.

must call for evidence on the physical interdependencies among water users; and the state engineer, the petitioner, and any protestors may give evidence. The final decision is determined by the court.

To the extent that rights are defined in terms of the quantity of water diverted, third-party impairment is a real problem. The question is which mechanism best solves the problem. Seastone and Hartman compared the judicial to the administrative process in the allocation of water among competing uses: "The logic of the systems suggests that the administrative process of water allocation has provided a closer approximation to efficiency criteria than has emerged from the judicial process."[20] The basic difference can be attributed to the administrative agencies' use of engineering data, procedures, and personnel, while the courts "relegate the engineering skills to a minor role."[21] In other words, the administrative approach enables state engineers to dispassionately allocate water in a way that closely approximates efficiency. But is there an alternative definition of water rights that can eliminate the need for either judicial or administrative review and leave the determination of changes in use or diversion up to the market process? This question will be addressed later in this chapter.

Federal Reclamation Water Use

When the Bureau of Reclamation entered the water storage and delivery business in 1902, it began telling water users where, when, and how they could use the water. Since government money was being used to provide the water, politicians and bureaucrats claimed that they had a right to influence water allocation. The initial Reclamation Act of 1902 required that funds for the construction of dams and delivery of water be repaid within 10 years, and the period of federal control was relatively limited. But as the rent-seeking process encouraged the eventual extension of repayment periods to over 50 years, federal control was expanded and strengthened. To complicate reclamation restrictions even more, the Bureau of Reclamation obtains water from the state and sells it to an irrigation or conservancy district, which delivers it to a final user.

Charles Meyers and Richard Posner have pointed out the extent of the Bureau of Reclamation's control over transfers:

> Even after repayment of its loans, the Bureau, it appears, retains title

[20]D. A. Seastone and L. M. Hartman, "Alternative Institutions for Water Transfers: The Experience in Colorado and New Mexico," *Land Economics* 39 (February 1963): 43.
[21]Ibid.

to the dams and reservoirs constructed under the project and with them title to project water. In addition, many pay-out projects have rehabilitation contracts with the Bureau, which give it a continuing interest in the financial integrity of the project. The Bureau's interest in projects that have not paid out is clear, since it looks to the individual farmers or to the district . . . for recovery of the costs allocated to irrigation. At all events, whether by statute, expressed or implied contract, general understanding based on past and expected future favors, or some combination of these, the Bureau's consent must be obtained for the transfer of any significant quantity of water, supplied by either a paid-out or nonpaid-out project, where the transfer involves either use on a different parcel of land or a different use; and this is so whether the transfer is within or outside project boundaries. Although substantial transfers have been proposed and some approved, neither the reclamation statutes nor Bureau rules contain precise criteria for when consent should be granted or withheld.[22]

The potential for rent seeking in this system is great. Bureaucrats can retain budget and power through their authority to grant or restrict transfers. Water users have an incentive to expend effort and resources in attempts to influence Bureau of Reclamation decisions because they will affect their wealth positions. The magnitude of the rent-seeking potential is illustrated by recent court rulings on the delivery of Bureau of Reclamation water to farms larger than 160 acres. The Reclamation Act of 1902 provided that

no right to the use of water for land and private ownership shall be sold for a tract exceeding 160 acres to any one individual landowner, and no such sale shall be made to any landowner unless he be an actual bona fide resident on the land, or occupant thereof residing in the neighborhood.

This provision has been loosely interpreted so that Bureau of Reclamation water can be allocated to 320 acres of land jointly owned by a husband and wife. The Omnibus Adjustment Act of 1926, which required that excess land had to be sold if water from bureau projects was to be supplied, has been ignored.

As the optimal size of farms grew, Bureau of Reclamation water was transferred to owners of larger scale operations. By 1977, of 11 million acres of the irrigatable land that benefited from Bureau of Reclamation projects, nearly 2.3 million acres were classified as excess lands. Since

[22]Charles J. Meyers and Richard A. Posner, *Market Transfers of Water Rights,* Legal Study no. 4 (Washington, D.C.: National Water Commission, July 1, 1971), p. 20.

the initial legislation prohibited the transfer of water to farms with excess lands, the Bureau of Reclamation was clearly violating its charge.

In 1976, National Land for the People, Inc. filed suit against excess land sales in the Westlands Irrigation District. The group claimed that the bureau was violating the Reclamation Act of 1902 by delivering water to farms larger than 160 acres and by providing individuals and corporations—not small family farmers—with subsidies in excess of $1.4 million per farm.[23] National Land for the People successfully forced the Department of Interior to enforce the original limits of the act; but James Watt, then head of the Mountain States Legal Foundation, managed to have the regulations overturned on the grounds that an environmental impact statement was not filed. The Carter administration finally had the regulations reissued, but Watt, as Secretary of Interior, suspended them in February 1981, drafting instead legislation that amended the initial limitations. The legislation was passed in 1982, making it possible for the Bureau of Reclamation to deliver water to farms closer to the optimal size and, in effect, granting subsidies to larger landowners.

For the market to allocate water resources, rights to water must be well-established and transferable. Legal institutions have interfered with both. In order to obtain a permit to use water, an individual must demonstrate that the water will be put to a beneficial use, the determination of which is left to the political and judicial processes. Market criteria are not the determining factor. Restrictions are placed on inter- and intra-basin transfers of rights as well as on changes of use, which encourage rent seeking and distort the true opportunity cost of water. As a result, market failure is ensured.

Salvaging the System

To understand how some simple changes could improve the efficiency of water markets, consider the following hypothetical example (see figure 2).[24] The Gallison River is being used to supply water for municipal, agricultural, industrial, and recreational uses. The river is located in a Western state where the doctrine of prior appropriation evolved from early mining and farming interests. Average annual flow in the Gallison is 2,000 acre feet. First settlement along the river came in 1862 when Farmer Baden began supplying agricultural products to

[23]Ronald Brownstein and Nina Easton, "The Wet, Wet West," *Washington Monthly* 13 (November 1981): 42–49.

[24]For a similar example, see Meyers and Posner, pp. 9–14.

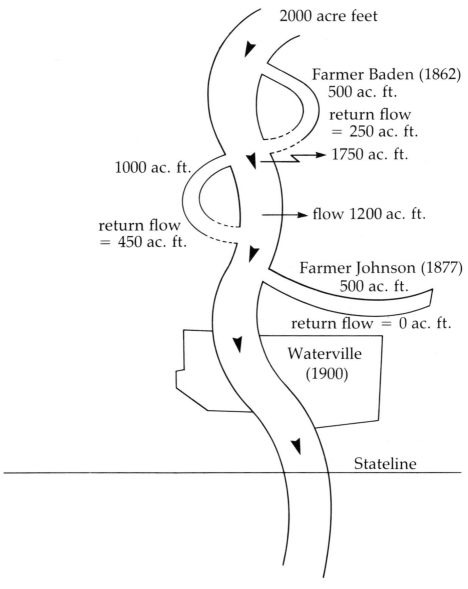

Figure 2

HYPOTHETICAL GALLISON RIVER
(prior to dam construction)

2000 acre feet

Farmer Baden (1862)
500 ac. ft.

return flow
= 250 ac. ft.

1750 ac. ft.

1000 ac. ft.

flow 1200 ac. ft.

return flow
= 450 ac. ft.

Farmer Johnson (1877)
500 ac. ft.

return flow = 0 ac. ft.

Waterville
(1900)

Stateline

nearby mining camps. At that time, he constructed an irrigation canal that diverted 500 acre feet of water from the stream. The crops he planted and the irrigation techniques he used resulted in a return flow of 250 acre feet. In 1872, Farmer Hill settled in the Gallison Valley and constructed his own canal, which withdrew 1,000 acre feet and returned 450 acre feet. The combination of withdrawals and return flows left 1,200 acre feet of water unclaimed. Farmer Johnson entered the valley in 1877 and claimed 500 acre feet, which he diverted through an ingenious canal system into the neighboring basins. Hence, the return flow from his withdrawal was zero.

By the time the town of Waterville was established in 1900, the procedure for establishing water rights had been turned over to district courts. The community's petition for a permit to use 500 acre feet for domestic consumption was not challenged. But when a cement plant located in the next basin petitioned the court for the remaining 200 acre feet and proposed transferring the water out of the Gallison Basin, the court refused on the grounds that such a transfer did not constitute a beneficial use for Gallison Valley residents. Eventually, the 200 acre feet were claimed by a downstream user in the next state.

The growth of Waterville led to an increase in municipal water demands. Since the river was completely appropriated, Waterville was forced to purchase rights from other users. When Waterville attempted to purchase the 200 acre feet from the user in the downstream state, that state's water engineer disapproved the transfer. Waterville then attempted to secure the water from upstream farmers but found them unwilling to sell at the price Waterville offered. The community exercised condemnation procedures to obtain the 200 acre feet desired and successfully obtained the water at the price originally offered. Farmer Johnson then attempted to purchase 1,000 acre feet of water from Farmer Hill. The court refused his petition, arguing that withdrawal of 1,000 acre feet with no return flow would impair third parties downstream and that a transfer out of the basin would not be a beneficial use.

To further complicate water rights in the Gallison Valley, Baden, Hill, and Johnson formed the Gallison Conservancy District and lobbied for congressional authorization to construct a Bureau of Reclamation dam on Bureau Creek. Since the creek was not appropriated, construction of the irrigation dam would not cause third-party impairment. In 1935, congressional approval of funds for dam construction was forthcoming, with the standard provision that the funds be repaid by the conservancy district. An interest charge of 3 percent was established, but bad crops and low prices led the Bureau of Reclamation to grant several grace periods. Until repayment was completed, the bureau would retain ownership of the water, even though the farmers owned transferable shares in the conservancy district.

After several bad years, Farmer Hill decided to sell his shares in the district to Waterville in order to avoid bankruptcy. The Bureau of Reclamation protested Hill's petition on the grounds that the contract between the bureau and the conservancy district only allows water to be used for agricultural purposes within the district. The bad economic conditions facing the farmers in the district, however, did lead to another grace period during which repayments were suspended.

The example illustrates how transfers are restricted. Everything from interstate to interbasin transfers to changes of use is brought before the judicial or administrative process before they are allowed. Could these transfers be handled through the market mechanism? When the cement plant petitioned for unclaimed water to transfer to the next basin, the market signal was that this use was of higher value than other uses. There is no reason to suspect that market signals could not determine whether this constituted a beneficial use. It is easy to understand, however, why Gallison Valley residents might protest the transfer to keep the water in their basin *in case* they might want it in the future. By limiting competition from outside sources, water prices will be kept lower for users in the basin.

Waterville's attempt to obtain additional water through market exchanges also seems acceptable. If a downstream user in another state were willing to sell to Waterville, the implication is that municipal uses have a higher value than agricultural uses to the extent that the political process reflects municipal value. In this case, there seems to be no economic (efficiency) rationale for banning interstate transfers. Upstream users were unwilling to sell their water at the price being offered by Waterville, suggesting that agricultural values to them were greater than the municipal value. By allowing Waterville to condemn rights, either water was being transferred to a lower valued use or Waterville residents were obtaining their water for a price that was less than they were willing to pay. In the first case, inefficiency results; in the second, value (rents) is transferred from farmers to municipal residents.

Farmer Hill's attempt to sell his shares in the conservancy district also reflects an efficient water transfer. It is reasonable that the Bureau of Reclamation would want to protect its interest in having the construction costs repaid, but such restrictions on transfer reduce the likelihood of repayment. If Farmer Hill had been allowed to sell his shares and, hence, his water to a user who valued the water more, it is more likely that repayment would occur.

> A flat prohibition against transfers, however, is unnecessary. The Bureau's interest would be adequately protected by a rule that any purchaser of project water must assume payment of that portion of the outstanding construction obligation allocated to the water transferred and give security for a share of the O & M charges if the transfer diminishes the ability of the remaining users to pay them. Upon satisfactory arrangements being made by the purchaser with the Bureau for such payments, the Bureau should be required to consent to the transfer.[25]

From a rent-seeking perspective, it is easy to understand why the Bureau of Reclamation might want to prohibit transfers, even if grace periods are necessary. By extending the pay-out period, the bureau retains control of the project and of the water. Repayment simply returns funds to the general treasury, which is a common pool, and at the same time reduces the power of the bureaucracy. In short, there seems to be no economic rationale for the restrictions suggested in this example.

What about restrictions that alter the return flow and impact on downstream users? Can a case be made that state intervention is necessary when return flows are altered by changes in use or in diversion? Throughout the economic literature,

> externalities resulting from ill-defined property rights are viewed as arising because water can be used and reused along a stream basin. Transfer by one individual can affect the return flow available to others. To prevent damage to third parties, earlier writers on this subject such as Meyers and Posner called for establishing property rights in return flows. The notion exists that externalities dominate water-resource allocation and that legal impediments to efficient water transfer are far too abundant.[26]

Judicial and administrative frameworks are supposed to eliminate these externalities, but, as we have seen, they have allowed for a greater degree of rent seeking.

The problem of third-party impairment due to alterations in return flows can all but be eliminated by defining water rights in terms of consumption rather than diversion. Under such a system, if a person

---

[25]Ibid., p. 22.

[26]Ronald N. Johnson and Michael Warner, "The Definition of a Surface Water Right and Transferability," *Journal of Law and Economics* 14 (October 1981): 273–74.

diverts 100 acre feet and returns 40 acre feet, he has a right to transfer only 60 acre feet. This system has two advantages. First, it eliminates the return flow problem, since only the amount consumed can be transferred. If the point of diversion or the use of 60 acre feet is changed, no other parties are affected since no other parties have any right to the 60 acre feet. Second, consumptive rights encourage water conservation. The individual with the right to transfer the 60 acre feet has an incentive to discover conservation measures. By reducing the consumptive use coefficient, the owner can free up water to be used elsewhere.

This assumes that flow constraints on the water system are not binding. If during a low water year there is insufficient water to meet all demands, a change in the point of diversion or use can have third-party effects.

> With a flow constraint binding at, say, point i, the transfer of a water right from some point i to a point above must result in reduced stream flows at i. This would imply that the stream flow at that point is no longer commensurate with the consumptive-use right held by user i. Note that the resulting impairment is due to a change in location to an upstream point. A downstream transfer will not cause third-party impairment as long as consumptive-use rights are not exceeded.[27]

This impairment is a function of the stream flow relative to the amount of diversion at various points along the stream. Therefore, the impairment will be site specific. "Impairment, then, is likely to be more of a local than general issue and one that involves attempts to move a right upstream."[28] Under these conditions, the judicial or administrative process will have to correct the problem. Note, however, that the role of governmental agencies in this situation is much less than it is under the current system. More decisions are being made in the market.

Colorado and New Mexico provide two examples of how consumptive-use rights have evolved. In Colorado, the owner is not entitled to transfer the quantity of water appropriated but is allowed to transfer the "duty of water." The Colorado Supreme Court has defined this duty as

> that measure of water, which, by careful management and use, without wastage, is reasonably required to be applied to any given tract of land for such period of time as may be adequate to produce therefrom a maximum amount of such crops as ordinarily are grown thereon.

[27]Ibid., p. 279.
[28]Ibid., p. 283.

It is not a hard and fast unit of measurement, but is variable according to conditions. . . .[29]

Technical data, such as those found in table 7, can be useful in determining the consumptive-use right. For example, when the city of Denver sought to purchase water rights whose appropriated total was nearly 400 cubic feet per second, the Colorado court allowed only the transfer of 80 cubic feet per second.[30] Unfortunately, even though the Colorado courts recognize consumptive-use rights, they have not allowed individuals who conserve water to transfer it. This gives individual water users little incentive to develop new technologies that reduce the consumptive-use coefficients.

New Mexico has performed better. The state water engineer is charged with adjudicating water rights to eliminate third-party impairments, so transfers are only allowed on the basis of consumptive use. For example, when the Public Service Company of New Mexico purchased 10.23 acre feet and changed both location and use of the water, the state engineer wrote in the "Dedication of Water Rights" document:

> (2) This dedication is for 6.82 acres of irrigated land having a diversion right of 20.46 acre feet of water per anum and having a consumptive use of 1.5 acre feet per irrigated acre for a total of 10.23 acre feet per anum for consumptive use.[31]

Such a specific definition of rights is common in the New Mexico system.

New Mexico's state engineer also appears to recognize the problem of binding flow constraints. In a case involving a small stream subject to constraints,

> the hearing examiner concluded that an unrestricted change in location of withdrawals would have impaired existing users located above the existing well but below the proposed well. In particular, the examiner found the flows would not be ample during a dry part of the year. . . . The recommendation that withdrawals at the new location be limited during the period June 16 to September 30 does not imply that the total consumptive use of the applicants had to be reduced. The examiner's report explicitly stated that the applicants could exercise their rights by making withdrawals from the existing well during

---

[29]Quoted in Timothy D. Tregarthen, "Water in Colorado: Fear and Loathing of the Marketplace," in *Water Rights: Scarce Resource Allocation, Bureaucracy, and the Environment*, Terry L. Anderson, ed. (Cambridge, Mass.: Ballinger Press, 1983).

[30]Hartman and Seastone, *Water Transfers*, pp. 23–24.

[31]Quoted in Johnson and Warner, p. 285.

Table 7

SEASONAL CONSUMPTIVE USE CROP COEFFICIENTS FOR IRRIGATION

Crop	Consumptive-use coefficient*
Alfalfa	0.80 to 0.90
Bananas	.80 to 1.00
Beans	.60 to .70
Cocoa	.70 to .80
Coffee	.70 to .80
Corn (Maize)	.75 to .85
Cotton	.60 to .70
Dates	.65 to .80
Flax	.70 to .80
Grains, small	.75 to .85
Grain, sorghums	.70 to .80
Oilseeds	.65 to .75
Orchard crops:	
Avocado	.50 to .55
Grapefruit	.55 to .65
Orange and lemon	.45 to .55
Walnut	.60 to .70
Deciduous	.60 to .70
Pasture crops:	
Grass	.75 to .85
Ladino whiteclover	.80 to .85
Potatoes	.65 to .75
Rice	1.00 to 1.10
Soybeans	.65 to .70
Sugar beets	.65 to .75
Sugarcane	.80 to .90
Tobacco	.70 to .80
Tomatoes	.65 to .70
Truck crops, small	.60 to .70
Vineyard	.50 to .60

SOURCE: U.S. Department of Agriculture, "Irrigation Water Requirements" (Washington, D.C.: U.S. Government Printing Office, 1971), p. 11.

*The lower values are for the more humid areas, and the higher values are for the more arid climates.

that period. In essence, the state engineer's ruling called for modification of the transfer and not an absolute ban on it. Furthermore, it is apparent that impairment in La Jara Creek case was both site-specific and the impaired parties identifiable.[32]

Summary

The belief that the doctrine of appropriation contains a great deal of potential for market failure appears to be unfounded. Water quality and instream use do generate some special problems, but a system of well-established and transferable property rights generally promotes efficient water allocation. The allocation problems in many Western states are not the fault of the doctrine of appropriation as much as they are the fault of restrictions placed on water markets. Administrative agencies and courts continually interfere with what constitutes a water right and, hence, with the definition and enforcement of those rights. Furthermore, nearly all states restrict transfers through the judicial or administrative process so that the potential for rent seeking arises and inefficiency is generated.

To salvage the appropriation doctrine, many of the restrictions on water transfers must be removed. When the diversion and use of water cannot be changed, higher valued alternatives are foregone at a cost to both the water owner and society. If Northern California water owners could sell their rights to Southern California municipalities, it is likely that water with low marginal value in agriculture would be shifted to the higher marginal valued municipal uses, again assuming that the political process is reflecting correct values. Even if there is governmental failure, at least the politicians and bureaucrats are facing a positive price (opportunity cost) as opposed to a zero price if taking is allowed. Ignoring federal subsidies and environmental effects, the Peripheral Canal debate in California could have been defused if water rights could be bought and sold. Similarly, water shortages in the Colorado River Basin could be more easily solved if rights were transferable.

Burness and Quirk "assert that often what appears to be a shortage of water is actually the manifestation of restrictions on water rights transfer."[33] In the Colorado River case, the Metropolitan Water District in Southern California stands to lose large quantities of water as a result

---

[32]Ibid., pp. 286–87.

[33]H. Stuart Burness and James P. Quirk, "Water Laws, Water Transfers, and Economic Efficiency: The Colorado River," *Journal of Law and Economics* 23 (April 1980): 133.

of their low priority rights and of Mexican claims. "A potential supply source exists among the water users in the Imperial and Coachella irrigation districts. . . . However, existing California statutes preclude the transfer of water outside irrigation districts; one would hope enabling legislation would be quickly forthcoming. . . ."[34]

If irrigators could sell their water, they would have to consider alternative irrigation technologies and cropping patterns, and they would have the incentive to do so if rights were transferable. Salvaging the appropriations doctrine does not require new institutions but, rather, the elimination of existing restrictions on the market. Establishing institutions similar to those in New Mexico would foster more efficient water allocation. The problem is that existing bureaucratic agencies lose power when allocation is turned over to the market process. For water markets to develop, ideas must change and new political coalitions must reduce the power of bureaucracies. When this happens, the appropriations doctrine will provide the institutional foundation for a relatively efficient water market.

[34]Ibid.

VI. Privatizing Instream Flows

When the doctrine of appropriation was evolving in the American West, there was little need to consider who had the rights to instream flows. The primary demands for water involved diverting it for mining or agricultural purposes, and flows were usually adequate to meet the demands. The only instream use of any consequence was navigation, and initially such use was negligible. But as people began using streams for everything from piloting paddle wheelers to floating logs, demand increased; and users began insisting that the necessary levels of water must be maintained. To ensure that this demand was met, the commerce clause of the Constitution was invoked to prevent users from interfering with interstate commerce on rivers.

Over time, the demand for instream uses grew to include waste disposal and recreation. Industrialization meant that effluent was discharged into rivers and lakes, and with rising incomes and leisure time, aesthetic values were increasing. Instream uses began to compete directly with diversion uses, making it impossible for the institutional structure to ignore rights to instream flows. Judicial and administrative agencies responded to changing relative values by instituting new rules to govern instream use. Is the collective action that has been used to resolve instream versus diversion uses necessary? Can markets be allowed to resolve the conflicts?

Before answering these questions, it is important to recognize that instream uses have two dimensions. The first deals with the quantity of water available for recreation, fishing, water fowl, and scenic purposes. The second concerns the quality of water available for downstream users. Because water flows downhill, it is a natural medium for disposing of effluent at no cost to the polluter. Unfortunately, as the flow of water decreases, the ability of the stream to assimilate the effluent declines, increasing the cost of pollution to downstream users. As institutional changes for improving the market allocation of water are debated, both the quantity and quality aspects of instream flows must be considered.

The Public Good Argument

Most people consider instream flows to be a public good, so institutional arrangements for allocating the flows came to depend on collective action. Economists argue that there are two aspects of goods that render them public and, therefore, subject to collective rather than private provision. First, nonpaying users cannot be excluded from consuming the good. Second, once the good is provided to one individual it can be provided to others at no additional cost. Consider the consequences of these two arguments.

If nonpaying users cannot be excluded from consuming the good, private firms will have no incentive to produce it, since the firm would incur some costs but would receive little or no revenue. The extent of this problem centers on the cost of enforcing a property right. A rancher who owns a large section of land along a fishing stream may find it costly to deny fishermen access if they do not pay. Fences, signs, and game wardens provide some measure of enforcement, but they also cost money. Whether they cost too much and prevent private production is an empirical question. Certainly it is more costly to exclude nonpaying fishermen from a section of a stream than it is to exclude nonpaying consumers from eating the bread produced by a bakery. As we shall see, there is evidence that enforcement costs may not be so high that they preclude private production of certain instream uses. Private producers have refused to provide more instream uses because existing laws do not allow them to charge for the services of their streams.

There is a more difficult exclusion problem with respect to the scenic value of a stream. When a traveler on a public highway enjoys the sight of a beautiful stream surrounded by changing fall colors, there is little doubt that the view provides positive value. The owner of the land and water resources that provide the view would be hard-put to collect from every traveler who enjoys the scene. Public highways make the exclusion costs very high in this case and, therefore, create a positive benefit for nonpaying consumers.

To compound the problem, it is argued that an existence value can be associated with many amenities; that is, some people derive satisfaction from simply knowing that the amenity is there. A New Yorker may be happy knowing that a wilderness area exists in Alaska, even if he has no intention of ever visiting it. He receives a positive value from the amenity without paying for it, and it is impossible to prevent him from enjoying its existence value. The argument is not unique to amenity resources; its logic can also be applied to many privately produced goods. A discussion of existence demands at a staff meeting of the U.S. Fish and Wildlife Service demonstrates how far the argument can be pushed:

> One of the staff people said, "I feel very strongly about wilderness even though I may never visit one of these areas. I want to know that people can enjoy that kind of resource, that it is there, and that it is preserved and is available even though I may never be able to use it myself." One of the other participants responded, "That's strange— I feel the same way about Raquel Welch."[1]

There is an element of existence value with any good, but it does not preclude private production of that good.

The argument that a public good is one that once it is supplied to one individual it can be supplied to others at no additional cost relates closely to scenic and existence values. Providing the view of a beautiful river to one individual does not preclude another from consuming it. Economic efficiency dictates that goods should be priced according to the marginal or additional cost of producing them; and since the additional cost of providing the view for an extra person is zero, the implication is that a zero price is efficient. Under these conditions, however, a private producer is unable to achieve a rate of return necessary to stimulate production. The classic example in economics is the lighthouse. It was argued that once the lighthouse was built and lighting the way for passing ships, the additional cost of guiding another ship was zero. As Ronald Coase has pointed out, however, private lighthouses have been in existence for many years and innovative contractual arrangements have evolved to allow private entrepreneurs the return necessary to produce the service.[2]

While instream uses of water may have some public good characteristics, it does not necessarily follow that private markets cannot provide those uses. The free rider problem can be overcome by innovative contractual arrangements; private groups, such as Trout Unlimited, Ducks Unlimited, and The Nature Conservancy, have demonstrated that private resources can be devoted to the provision of some public

---

[1]Lynn A. Greenwalt, "Natural Resource Perspectives," in *Proceedings of the Symposium and Specialty Conference on Instream Flow Needs*, J. F. Orsborn and C. H. Allman, eds., vol. 2 (Bethesda, Md.: American Fisheries Society, 1976), p. 622.

[2]R. H. Coase, "The Lighthouse in Economics," *Journal of Law and Economics* 17 (October 1974): 257–76.

goods. The major stumbling block to the private provision of instream uses is the existing legal structure.

Public and Private Alternatives for Instream Flows

Since most Western states have granted only usufructuary rights to water, declaring that the water belongs to the state, and since instream uses have some public good characteristics, it should not be surprising that the standard approaches to the maintenance of instream flows have involved public action. States have most commonly used some form of water reservation to ensure instream flows, relying on legislation, bureaucratic action, or purchases of water rights to set water aside for instream purposes.

In an attempt to head off an initiative that proposed setting minimum stream flows on all rivers and streams, the Idaho state legislature passed a law in 1978 that established base flows on the Snake River and authorized the Idaho Water Resources Board to appropriate water to ensure instream uses. Under the law, the board may either initiate action or respond to private requests for instream reservations; its actions are subject to legislative approval and must not interfere with vested water rights. While actions of the board are subject to technical constraints, such as past flow records and minimum flows necessary for the preservation of fish and wildlife habitat, recreation, navigation, aesthetic beauty, and water quality, the board still has a great deal of discretion to act in the public interest. To date, the board's actions have been confined to noncontroversial streams, but the political nature of the reservation process would make it difficult for the board to reserve instream flows where agricultural and mining interests are active.

> Hence it is unlikely that the Idaho approach to instream flow preservation will result in the protection of flows in the more populous and developed areas of the state. If such streams are protected, it will be a result of the ability of those valuing instream water uses to garner the necessary political power in the state legislature.[3]

The state of Washington attempts to maintain its instream flows through its Department of Ecology, which has the power to deny or make conditional permits for water appropriation. The department has effectively used its power to close 250 streams to consumptive appropriations. In 1969, the Washington legislature gave the board the added

[3]James Huffman, "Instream Water Use: Public and Private Alternatives," in *Water Rights: Scarce Resource Allocation, Bureaucracy, and the Environment,* Terry L. Anderson, ed. (Cambridge, Mass.: Ballinger Press, 1983).

authority to establish minimum stream flow requirements for wildlife habitat, recreation, and environmental purposes. By 1980, the Department of Ecology had received 26 requests from the Department of Fisheries and the Department of Game to establish minimum flows, but only one of the requests had been acted on. The lack of action can be attributed to a 1971 statute that requires the Department of Ecology to set base flows for all perennial rivers and streams. Base flows specify the quantity of water necessary to sustain a stream during extended periods without precipitation. The department must collect and analyze historical stream flow records and apply technical expertise to the data. Unlike the Idaho system, where politics plays an important role, the Washington system depends primarily on technical experts. Except for the provision to waive base flow requirements when hydroelectric power is threatened, there is little room in the Washington system for economic criteria in the establishment of instream flows.

Montana maintains instream flows by reserving water from private appropriation. The 1973 Water Use Act authorizes federal, state, and local governments to apply to the Department of Natural Resources and Conservation (DNRC) for water reservations for existing or future beneficial uses or to maintain minimum flows. The DNRC's most ambitious undertaking was its consideration of Yellowstone River reservations:

> Because private water users could not apply for reservations, the board sought to assure that the reservations that it granted did not tie up all of the water and thus prohibit any future private development of water. However, the variable nature of the stream flow and the inadequacy of much of the data available to the board raises some doubt about the prospects for future private water development. . . . Of course the board granted numerous other reservations for consumptive water uses by municipalities and agriculturalists, but by far the lion's share of the water was reserved for instream flows.[4]

Under this system, again there is little use of economic criteria and not much flexibility once the reservations are made.

In Colorado, the Colorado Water Conservation Board applies for unappropriated rights or purchases existing rights; the board is specifically forbidden to acquire rights by eminent domain. The Colorado system has two important characteristics: First, like any other appropriator, the board must have evidence that its requests for water constitute a beneficial use. Second, when the board purchases existing

4Ibid.

rights, it must pay the market rate and, hence, the opportunity cost. While the state's budget constraint is considerably different from that of any private user, the system does force the state to consider the costs of instream flows. In a state such as Colorado, where most water rights have already been claimed, the market approach is probably the only viable alternative to state action.

Comparing these four methods of maintaining instream flows provides insights into whether governmental action helps promote efficiency. The Idaho, Washington, and Montana systems exclude some waters from private appropriation or directly regulate existing rights. To the extent that water cannot be appropriated, these systems depend on "wise administrators" who must know how much water should be withheld from private appropriation and the appropriate uses of that water. The system is obviously fraught with the many problems of governmental failure (see chapter II). Even where administrators or legislators are not subject to political pressures, it is unlikely that they will have enough information to make efficient trade-offs among water uses. In the absence of prices, values are difficult, if not impossible, to determine.

Efficiency is further impeded because administrators and legislators do not have to face the opportunity costs of their actions. When water is reserved for instream uses so that consumptive uses are precluded, the decision-makers do not have to consider the foregone alternatives. To complicate the process, agricultural, mining, industrial, and municipal users will compete with instream users to make their political voices heard. There is no guarantee, however, that political expressions of preference will mirror economic values. Regulating existing rights through restrictions on transfers constitutes a taking in much the same way that zoning does. The Colorado approach has a slight advantage over the others in that it forces voters, legislators, and bureaucrats to at least indirectly consider the opportunity costs of instream uses. As long as existing consumptive rights must be purchased, state revenues will have to be provided. Nevertheless, it is important to remember that the state budget is a common pool, and individuals seeking revenues to purchase water rights will still be able to ignore the full opportunity costs of their actions.[5] It should also be remembered that decision-makers determine future as well as present water use and that in order to do so they must be able to accurately predict future values of

[5]John Baden and Rodney Fort, "Natural Resources and Bureaucratic Predators," *Policy Review* 11 (Winter 1980): 69–82.

water in a changing world. Once water is reserved for instream uses, they will find it difficult to alter that use unless there is overwhelming evidence that values have changed. No existing system provides the dynamic elements of a marketplace, where uses change continually in response to changes in relative values.

The governmental regulation of instream flows has been rationalized on the basis of market imperfections. It is assumed that private individuals or corporations cannot capture a sufficient return from providing instream uses and, therefore, markets will not promote an efficient amount of flows. The only reasonable solution, it is argued, is for the state to intervene and ensure an efficient quantity of instream water. As we have seen, however, it is questionable whether governmental intervention can come any closer than markets to promoting efficiency. When prices do not exist, values are difficult to determine; when voluntary trades do not determine use, opportunity costs are ignored; and when the political process is used to determine allocation, well-organized special interests tend to preempt diffuse general interests.

Even if governmental allocation could improve efficiency, the costs of state transactions would be considerable. As long as the state has discretion over water rights allocation, individuals will attempt to obtain favorable treatment. When a governmental agency uses regulations to take rights from one individual and give them to another, a transfer has been effected. To influence the outcome, people will neglect productive activities and invest in transfer activities. Idaho's legislative process encourages people with an interest in water allocation to try to influence their legislators. The reservation process in Montana is extremely costly when viewed in terms of the time and money spent on hearings and court cases. Under these systems, the cooperation found in the marketplace is replaced with challenge and conflict, and what could be a productive enterprise is transformed into a negative-sum game.

Examples of Markets

If we are to be convinced that markets provide the best alternative for allocating instream flows, it is reasonable to ask how efficient the market actually is. There is little doubt that if private individuals or corporations cannot define, enforce, and transfer rights to instream uses, water for such uses will not be provided in very large quantities. In light of rising amenity values, why are private individuals incapable of defining and enforcing rights to instream flows? The answer may be

that existing inefficiencies in water allocation result from deficiencies in the private rights system rather than from alleged market failures. The existing water loss seriously limits private acquisition of instream flow rights, so we cannot be sure from experience that the initial public-good assumption is accurate.[6]

In general, market failure refers to situations where property rights are *not* well-defined, enforced, or transferable. Since the task of defining and enforcing property rights is largely governmental, it is odd that an insufficient property rights structure is referred to as market failure. It is more appropriate to refer to situations where property rights are not well specified as cases of governmental or institutional failure.

In many Western states, the institutional (legal and judicial) structure precludes the private ownership of instream flows. In some cases, the concept of beneficial use, which was initially developed for agricultural, mining, and domestic uses, does not include instream flows. In the early mining camps, beneficial use was determined by any user who was willing to divert the water. Over time, however, beneficial use has been increasingly determined by judicial and administrative agencies, which have ruled that reserving instream flows for amenity purposes does not constitute a beneficial use. The requirement that diversion of water is necessary if a use is to be considered beneficial has produced perverse results. For example, when the Colorado legislature authorized the Colorado River Conservation District to reserve water for instream purposes in any natural stream large enough to support a fish population, the Colorado Supreme Court ruled that there was "no support in the law of this state for the proposition that a minimum flow of water may be 'appropriated' in a natural stream for piscatorial purposes without diversion of any portion of the water 'appropriated' from the natural course of the stream."[7] A much earlier case in a Utah court ruled on the disputed ownership of instream flows for the purpose of supporting a duck population. The court found that it was

> utterly inconceivable that a valid appropriation of water can be made under the laws of this state, when the beneficial use of which, after the appropriation is made, will belong equally to every human being who seeks to enjoy it. . . . [W]e are decidedly of the opinion that the beneficial use contemplated in making the appropriation must be one that insures to the exclusive benefit of the appropriator and subject to his dominion and control.[8]

[6]Huffman.

[7]Quoted in ibid.

[8]*Lake Shore Duck Club* v. *Lake View Duck Club,* 50 Utah 76, 309 (1917).

This suggests that the state was unwilling to allow individuals or groups to appropriate rights for the "public good." As long as the maintenance of instream flows does not constitute a beneficial use of water, private appropriators will not be able to define and enforce rights to the flows and a market cannot develop. Again, this is not a case of market failure but of governmental or institutional failure.

As long as use requires diversion, there is no way that property rights can be established for instream purposes. In most states, rights are forfeited if the water is not used; that is, if water is left in a stream to provide a nice view or a fish habitat. The law of abandonment is related to the beneficial use standard and was partly designed to prevent speculation in water. For example, if an individual were to appropriate water from a stream in the hope that its future value would rise, the water was not being used. The argument was that speculation in water caused valuable resources to remain idle and unproductive, inhibiting economic growth. Since the individual appropriating the rights bears the full opportunity cost of not consuming the water, however, the argument makes little sense from an efficiency perspective. Furthermore, water held for speculative purposes cannot be distinguished from water held for instream uses. Hence, the law of abandonment stifles the establishment of instream water rights and discourages what may be a highly valued use.

Both the beneficial use standard and the law of abandonment block the establishment of rights to instream flows and, therefore, encourage the common pool problem. As long as rights to the instream flows cannot be defined and enforced, markets cannot provide instream uses. The best solution is to eliminate beneficial use standards and laws of abandonment, thereby eliminating the institutional barrier to the efficient use of instream flows. The next best solution is to expand the beneficial use category to include more instream uses and to recognize that the nonuse of instream flows does not represent abandonment.

The evidence suggests that if legal obstacles to the establishment of instream rights were removed, private provision of instream uses would develop. On small streams, for example, where some of the legal restrictions do not apply, private owners are gainfully providing fishing. In the Yellowstone River Valley south of Livingston, Montana, several spring creeks begin and end on private land and are wholly appropriated by the landowners. Since access to the streams can be monitored inexpensively, landowners can collect a fee from fishermen. The fee, as much as $30 per day, gives the owners the incentive to develop spawning beds, prevent siltation, and keep cattle away from the streams to protect bank vegetation and cover. Owners limit the number of fishermen per day so that crowding does not diminish the value of the experience.

The Gallatin Valley to the west is another area noted for its excellent spring creek fishing. A few years ago, a recreational fisherman purchased some land and a stream that had been owned by a cattle rancher who had allowed his livestock to graze on the streambanks, which elminated vegetation and caused erosion. Because of such neglect, the size and number of trout in the stream were declining. The new owner got rid of the cattle, and in three years had reclaimed the stream and revived its fishing potential. The owner bears the cost of not using the land for cattle production, but he reaps the benefits of better fishing.

The results of private ownership of fishing rights are being noted all over the world. On the Southwest Miramichi River in Quebec, for example, the owner of a fishing camp has described how he turned his leased section into the perfect place for salmon fishing:

> I *made* it perfect by rafting a bulldozer in here. . . . We cleared away the gravel bar that kept fish from going up the tributary . . . dug the hundred-yard-long pool . . . and shoved a big-as-a-house boulder in place at the head of it. . . . With all due respect for Mother Nature, that pool was built by men and machines, and it seems to be as good now as it was the first year.[9]

In much the same way, Rich McIntyre, founder of Timberland Reclamations, Inc., in Bozeman, Montana, is improving neglected trout streams. By installing deflectors and wing dams, planting streambank vegetation, and creating other elements of trout habitat, McIntyre's company has increased the fishing quality and the aesthetic value of streams in the United States, Canada, and New Zealand, and his success is attracting other firms to the industry. Ed Zern has summarized the possibilities of using such reclamation efforts:

> So if you've sold your fleet of tankers to a Greek syndicate in order to have more time for fishing, Rich McIntyre's Timberland outfit can probably double the productivity of your Montana ranch. And if you don't have a tanker to your name, or even a rowboat, you can join your local angling club and help it use the same basic techniques to provide better fishing on public waters.[10]

All of these efforts, if they are to be successful, require some security of rights to instream flows.

[9]Quoted in Ed Zern, "Rx for Ailing Waters," *Field and Stream*, November 1982, p. 87.
[10]Ibid., p. 89.

The rights to instream flows in England and Scotland have long been well-established and encourage efficient instream uses. The tradition of trout fishing in Great Britain has led some owners to maintain their fisheries even though they have not marketed the fishing rights. As the value of fishing rights has risen with the demand, however, "there are few land owners . . . who can afford to ignore the commercial aspect of the sporting rights which they own."[11] As a result, many private, voluntary associations are developing. Angling associations have been formed to purchase rights to instream flows and charge for fishing:

> In the 1960s and 1970s smaller, privately managed fisheries that offered exclusivity in exchange for higher rod fees began to break out like an aquatic rash around [England]. Now every city and major town . . . has first-rate trout fishing within easy reach, and at an affordable price.[12]

In Scotland,

> virtually every inch of every major river and most minor ones is privately owned or leased, and while trespassing isn't quite as serious a crime as first-degree murder or high treason, it isn't taken lightly. . . . many of these stretches, which may be 100 yards of one bank of a river or several miles of both banks, are reserved years in advance, with a long waiting list.[13]

Even communities have recognized the value of fishing to the economy. In Grantown-on-Spey, the angler can

> join the local Angling Association by paying a weekly fee of about $25, and be free to fish any of seven miles of Association water. Sometimes, too, hotels and inns own or lease a stretch of river for their guests or can make arrangements with a local owner of fishing rights.[14]

When individuals or groups can own water for instream uses, they have an incentive to manage and improve the fishing habitat. In order to capture a return on their investments, owners must invest in enforcing their property rights, so the British hire private fish and game managers and invest in capital improvements on the streams.

[11]Douglas Southerland, *The Landowner* (London: Anthony Bond, 1968), p. 110.

[12]Brian Clarke, "The Nymph in Still Water," in *The Masters of Nymph,* J. M. Migel and L. M. Wright, eds. (New York: Nick Lyons Books, 1979), p. 219.

[13]Ed Zern, "By Your Boring Banks," *Field and Stream,* May 1981, p. 120.

[14]Ibid., pp. 120, 136.

To maintain their houses as homes, they retained housekeepers. To keep a proper garden and park, they had groundskeepers. Gamekeepers for stag and grouse. Then, as keepers of the kept, even gatekeepers to further secure things. And eventually, it was for the British to devise the ultimate in the art of maintenance—the riverkeeper.

Now, the name itself could easily be misinterpreted—as it has from time to time by our American "riverkeepers," whom we call "the Corps of Engineers." To keep a river from doing what it is supposed to do would be noxious to the British, as it is to many anglers.[15]

In the United States, where rights to instream flows cannot be established, having a private riverkeeper is unheard of; most people believe that this role must be left to the state. But when the role of riverkeeper is turned over to a governmental agency, such as the Bureau of Reclamation or the Corps of Engineers, the agency tends to "keep the river from doing what it is supposed to do."

Establishing private property rights generates many innovative ways of enforcing those rights. In England, for example,

one large estate owner . . . who was considerably troubled by poachers, solved his problem by inviting the most hardened poacher to form a fishing club, and provided two locks and a stretch of river for the purpose. It proved highly successful. The club members themselves contributed to the restocking of the water and the landowner's private rights were assiduously respected.[16]

As long as rights are well-defined, enforced, and transferable, entrepreneurs will arrive at new contractual arrangements to promote efficient allocation.

The British system illustrates how the United States might restructure its institutional arrangements to encourage the preservation of instream flows. Fishing rights in Scotland, for example, sell for as much as $220,000, giving stream owners an incentive to enhance instream flows.[17] To do otherwise would be to destroy wealth. Southerland has noted that there is no doubt

that sporting rights are a desirable amenity . . . but it must be remembered that without careful preservation much of the amenity would not exist. The good-natured farmer who allows anyone to shoot over his land, and does nothing to preserve his stocks, will soon find out

[15]Don Zahner, "Anglish Spoken Here," *Fly Fisherman* 12 (January 1980): 16.

[16]Southerland, pp. 114–15.

[17]Ed Zern, "Fishing Insurance: A Group Policy," *Field and Stream*, September 1981, p. 23.

there is nothing left to shoot. . . . [I]f he invests in improving his sporting amenities he is surely entitled to make what profit he can from his enterprise. That this should result in the rationing of the commodity by price is no more deplorable than the fact that Dover sole costs more than herring.[18]

Until rights to instream flows are allowed in the United States, property owners will have no reason to recognize these amenity values, authority will not be linked to responsibility, and efficient instream uses will not be encouraged.

Troublesome Pollution

There is perhaps no issue more troublesome to the property rights economist than air and water pollution. In both cases, the definition and enforcement of property rights are so costly that markets have not played a very important role in the allocation of resources used for waste disposal. While property rights to other aspects of water rights have been successfully established, there have been few cases where property rights have been granted to pollution or clean water.

If individuals own water in a stream and can use it for in- or out-of-stream purposes, it is possible that liability rules, which are a form of property rights, could be imposed. Owners of instream fishing rights, for example, could bring suit against a polluter upstream whose effluent adversely affects their fishing resource. In England, the Angler's Cooperative Association (ACA) has assumed the job of monitoring pollution:

> It has investigated nearly 700 pollution cases since it started and very rarely does it fail to get abatement or damages, as the case requires. These anglers have behind them a simple fact. Every fishery in Britain, except for those in public reservoirs, belongs to some private owner.[19]

These efforts have even preserved trout fishing on the Derwent River, which flows through the industrial city of Derby. The ACA successfully prevented the city from dumping sewage into the river and got an injunction against British Electric, preventing it from running warm water directly into the river. "The A.C.A. also deals with . . . mud running into a stream from a new road grade, or a ditch. . . . This is actually a good example of a common form of pollution which we accept but which is quite unnecessary and not hard to avoid."[20]

[18]Southerland, pp. 113–14.

[19]Douglas Clarke quoted in J. H. Dales, *Pollution, Property, and Prices* (Toronto: University of Toronto Press, 1968), p. 68.

[20]Quoted in ibid., p. 69.

In much the same way, when water is withdrawn from a stream for agricultural, industrial, or municipal uses, pollution raises the cost of using the water. The water must be cleaned up, and there are sufficient grounds to seek legal action against the polluter. Even in the late 1800s, the California Supreme Court recognized that individual polluters should be liable for their pollution.[21] When property rights for other uses of water are well-defined and enforced, however, it is easier for liability rules to be established and to control the level of pollution.

There are two situations, however, in which transaction costs reduce the feasibility of liability rules. First, where a large number of individuals live along a stream and suffer only a small amount of damage from the pollution, each individual tends to be a free rider in the legal action. If all individuals along the stream except one sue a polluter for damages, that one individual may enjoy a free ride; and since everyone has the same incentive to free ride, no legal action may be taken. Class action suits, of course, greatly reduce the magnitude of this problem, and associations are often formed to help overcome it. Property owner associations are common among landholders, and there is no reason to believe that they would be less common among water owners if property rights were well-defined and enforced. If transaction costs are high enough to prevent individuals along the stream from bringing suit jointly against the polluter, an argument can be made for intervention by a regulatory agency, such as the Environmental Protection Agency. One of the problems with governmental intervention, of course, is that special interest groups engaged in pollution are just as likely to influence the agency as are those who suffer the damages.

The second transaction cost arises when pollution is generated by more than one source. As long as water pollution comes from an easily identifiable source, such as a large municipal sewage or a large industrial plant, liability can be established. More commonly, however, pollution is generated by many individuals or groups along the stream. Under these conditions, separating out pollutants may be difficult, and the interaction of different pollutants may increase pollution costs. The problem is even more complicated when pollution comes from non-point sources, such as agriculture. When irrigation water carries pesticides and herbicides into a stream, it is very difficult to identify the source. While damages may be clear, liability rules will have little

[21]Charles W. McCurdy, "Stephen J. Field and Public Land Law Development in California, 1850–1866: A Case Study of Judicial Resource Allocation in Nineteenth-Century America," *Law and Society Review* 10 (Winter 1976): 262.

impact in these cases, since the liability cannot be assigned to a specific polluter. Even the successful Angler's Cooperative Association has failed to control pollution in those "cases where the polluter could not be identified."[22] In such cases, a well-defined and enforced system of water rights is unlikely to promote an optimal level of pollution, and a case can be made for some form of regulation.

Once the possibility of regulation is introduced, it is important to distinguish between optimality and efficiency.[23] We can conceptualize the optimal level of pollution by comparing its marginal benefits with its marginal costs (see figure 3).[24] The optimal level of pollution occurs at P*, where the additional benefits are exactly equal to the additional costs. Any more or less will result in a net social loss. If polluters who use the stream for waste disposal were liable for the cost of their pollution, they would have an incentive to choose pollution level P*. To pollute less would be to forego benefits that exceed costs, and to pollute more would be to incur costs that exceed benefits. In the absence of full liability, however, the polluter can enjoy the benefits of waste disposal without bearing all of the cost, and we can expect too much pollution.

When liability is too costly to assign, a regulatory agency is often called on to determine the optimal level of pollution. Unfortunately, it is easier to conceptualize what P* is than to actually measure it. State and federal environmental protection agencies expend considerable resources on cost-benefit analyses; but given the subjective nature of benefits and costs, there is little reason to believe that optimality can ever be achieved. When the possibility of special interests influencing the estimates of benefits and costs is introduced into the model, the likelihood of optimality is reduced even further. Whether direct regulation, effluent charges, or some other form of regulation is used, an optimal level of water pollution is not likely to result.

In the absence of optimality, one might hope for a second-best solu-

[22]Dales, p. 69.

[23]Jerome W. Milliman, "Can Water Pollution Policy Be Efficient?" Cato Journal 2 (Spring 1982).

[24]Discussion of the optimal level of pollution and efficiency in achieving pollution reduction assumes that the normative issue of the legitimacy of rights has been resolved. Thus, neither optimality nor efficiency is strictly a technical issue but depends, at least for starting points, on moral judgments about who should have what rights. After that decision has been made, they depend on subjective evaluations of benefits and costs. For further discussion of this issue, see Murray Rothbard, "Law, Property Rights, and Air Pollution," Cato Journal 2 (Spring 1982).

Figure 3
BENEFITS AND COSTS OF POLLUTION

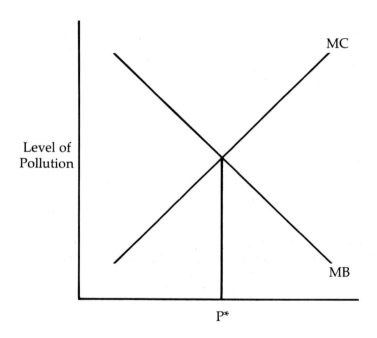

tion; that is, whatever level of pollution abatement is attained, it is attained at the lowest possible cost. Imagine several industrial plants, each discharging effluent into one stream. Assume that different technologies enable each firm to reduce effluent at a different cost. The optimal solution would be to achieve a pollution level of P* by having the polluters with the least-cost abatement technologies remove their pollution. If a regulatory agency attempts to legislate the solution, the problem becomes one of determining which firms can reduce pollution for the least cost.

To overcome this problem, market-like mechanisms, such as offsets, pollution banks, and tradable pollution rights, are being considered by pollution control agencies. Offsets permit some trading of pollution rights among established polluters and new or expanding firms, which have often been prohibited from polluting at all. Offsets allow those firms to pollute if they can prove that their pollution has been offset by reduced pollution elsewhere. Recently, for example, oil companies in the Santa Barbara channel have been allowed to increase their hydrocarbon emissions because they were able to decrease emissions from natural ocean sources.[25] Again, this encourages lower-cost abatement programs.

Pollution banking allows the intertemporal trading of pollution rights. By banking pollution control now, a firm can obtain a right to pollute more in the future, promoting efficiency over time as well as across space. This could mean that in an exceptionally profitable year, a firm might be willing to expend more on control in return for the right to control less in a bad year. Credits in the emission bank could even be sold to firms desiring to pollute at some time in the future.

Tradable pollution rights (sometimes referred to as bubbles) grant a certain amount of pollution in a stream basin or lake. Polluters are then allowed to increase pollution at some location in return for reducing pollution elsewhere. While the initial assignment of the rights will be controversial, the possibility of trading rights improves the likelihood of efficiency. If a right is held by a firm with low-cost abatement technology, the high-cost firm could be expected to purchase that right and the low-cost firm could be expected to use the proceeds to control pollution. This system is currently being applied in some airsheds with notable success. The value of the system is that once a pollution level has been determined, policymakers do not need information on the marginal cost of treatment at various locations.

[25]"Payoff from the Sea Floor," *Time*, October 11, 1982, p. 79.

Tradable pollution rights can reduce the costs of attaining a given level of pollution, but they can also affect the distribution of costs. For example, imagine a situation in which a downstream polluter at point A sells his pollution right to an upstream polluter at point B. The total level of pollution at point A would remain the same, and control would be achieved at a lower cost; but water users between point A and B would be at a disadvantage, since they will have more pollution flowing by them. The problem would no doubt be resolved by requiring state approval of all changes in the location of discharge. This solution, however, would be subject to the same problems that exist with approval for changes in use (see chapter V).

It is unlikely that existing regulatory institutions can determine the optimal level of pollution. Fortunately, there are mechanisms, such as offsets and tradable pollution rights, that can achieve a given level of pollution at a lower cost. Jerome Milliman has concluded that

> the evidence is fairly clear that the present policy of detailed direct regulation of discharges is expensive, wasteful, and ineffective. . . . Effective and efficient water pollution control policy requires a commitment to make greater use of the markets and the price system as instruments of the social policy. Even more basic, however, is a commitment to a goal of efficiency in environmental policy itself. The obstacles to such a commitment appear formidable.[26]

It is true that a greater commitment to markets could improve efficiency, but can we reasonably expect environmentalists, bureaucrats, and polluters to care about efficiency? Economic models assume that individuals in each of these groups are utility maximizers who have no proprietary interest in pursuing environmental efficiency for the public interest. Bureaucrats especially will be subject to intense special interest pressures that will cause them to diverge from the pursuit of socially efficient pollution control. Because governmental officials and bureaucrats increase their utility by expanding their spheres of influence, they have favored direct pollution control over market alternatives. The extent of discretionary power inherent in pollution regulation has been aptly summarized by Steven Williams:

> At every stage of the (regulation) procedure, we see government agencies exercising enormous discretion: The EPA sets standards for new plants in every subcategory of every industry; state agencies set standards for all plants to make them conform to the SIP (State Implementation Plans); state agencies decide whether or not to issue the

[26]Milliman, pp. 193–94.

necessary permits for a new plant in nonattainment or PSD (Preservation of Significant Deterioration) areas. This vast discretion has three dangerous facets: it is an occasion for influence-peddling, it breeds unfairness, and it erodes the rule of law.[27]

As long as direct regulation is used to control pollution levels, rent seeking in the form of influence peddling is likely to result. Markets for tradable pollution rights offer a viable alternative, but it would appear that there is little incentive for the regulators to adopt such solutions. Perhaps a greater commitment to markets will evolve as people begin to appreciate the market's ability to solve resource allocation problems. In the case of pollution, however, it is not sufficient to call for greater commitments to markets. We have not yet devised the property rights necessary to ensure an optimal and efficient allocation of water resources for use in pollution disposal. Perhaps water pollution presents a situation where collective action must be used. If this is the case, the focus must be on alternative collective institutions that can approximate the efficiency of markets.

Summary

State laws that prohibit the ownership of water for instream uses inhibit market solutions to instream use conflicts. With these prohibitions removed, we could move a long way toward efficient allocation and use. British water institutions, which promote a higher quality fishing experience and give owners an incentive to guard against stream pollution, suggest that markets can play a greater role.

The complete property rights and market solution to pollution must await the evolution of new property rights institutions. The current emphasis on direct regulation is expensive, wasteful, and ineffective; but market-like alternatives in the form of tradable pollution rights, offsets, and banking offer some hope for achieving more efficient control. Ironically, because they are more cost-effective and require less bureaucratic involvement, they have received little attention from policymakers.

[27]Steven F. Williams, "Pollution Control: Taxes Versus Regulation," Original paper 25, International Institute for Economic Research, August 1979, pp. 9–10.

VII. Groundwater Deeds

As with so many of our natural resources, there are growing concerns that groundwater supplies are being depleted by rapidly increasing demands. A *New York Times* article typifies the concern:

> In thirty years, drawing on a vast underground water formation called the Ogallala Aquifer, High Plains farmers have transformed the barren dust-bowl landscape into one of the richest agricultural regions of the world. Now, in many areas, the formation is nearly drained; everywhere the water table is dropping away from the irrigation pipes and pumps at a rate that has begun to frighten officials and farmers alike.[1]

The increased use of groundwater, however, is not confined to the Ogallala. In 1970, 19 percent of the water used in the United States came from groundwater sources. By 1980, reliance on groundwater had grown to 25 percent, and it is expected to continue growing. The West has become particularly dependent on groundwater use, where it accounts for 46 percent of municipal and 44 percent of industrial water supplies. Technology has also been influential in determining use rates. The development of sprinkler irrigation, for example, caused a threefold increase in groundwater withdrawals between 1950 and 1975 in the West. Today, these withdrawals account for 39 percent of all Western irrigation water used.

The increase in groundwater use might not be so worrisome if withdrawals from groundwater basins did not exceed natural recharge. But Kenneth Frederick has estimated that withdrawals exceed recharge in Western aquifers by more than 22 million acre feet each year.[2] Such mining has been particularly severe in the Ogallala Aquifer, which stretches from western Texas to northern Nebraska. In northern Texas and southwestern Oklahoma, withdrawals exceed recharge by 22 percent in normal years and 161 percent in dry years. For the North and

---

[1]"Depletion of Underground Water Formation Imperils Vast Farming Region," *New York Times*, April 11, 1981, p. B4.

[2]Kenneth D. Frederick, "The Future of Western Irrigation," *Southwestern Review of Management* 1 (Spring 1981): 21.

South Platte Basin, the percentages are 40 and 60, respectively.[3] To date, withdrawals constitute a small percentage of the total water stored in the Ogallala Aquifer; but groundwater use is growing rapidly, and the aquifer is being mined as a result.

The federal government has responded to the problem of groundwater mining in the same way it responded to surface water problems: It has attempted to increase water supplies. In 1976, Congress passed Public Law 94-587 (Sec. 193), authorizing $6 million

> to study the depletion of natural resources of those regions of the States of Colorado, Kansas, New Mexico, Oklahoma, Texas, and Nebraska presently utilizing the declining water resources of the Ogallala Aquifer, and to develop plans to increase water supplies in the area and report thereon to Congress, together with any recommendations for further Congressional action.

Because of this legislation, farmers have received funds to install dikes and dams to catch run-off and to experiment with other methods of increasing the supply of groundwater. Responding to these efforts and to proposed interbasin tranfers of water, Colorado Governor Richard D. Lamm stated, "I passionately believe the day of such large-scale technological solutions is coming to an end. We cannot produce our way out of a water crisis any more than we can produce our way out of an energy crisis. What we should have learned by now is that we must work on the demand side."[4]   While Governor Lamm may be mistaken about our ability to produce our way out of an energy crisis, he is certainly correct about our inability to solve groundwater problems by increasing supplies. The crisis in groundwater, as in surface water, is related to the institutional and legal framework. Without the proper information and incentives, private users are not likely to augment groundwater supplies or to reduce their demands on groundwater basins. The institutions that currently provide the information and incentives are a combination of property rights and central, bureaucratic agencies that dictate water allocation. When groundwater was abundant, the nature of these institutions made little difference; but growing demand has placed the claims on groundwater basins in direct competition with one another. Problems with drawdown, land subsidence, saltwater intrusion, and pumping costs all suggest the need for institutional reform. As the use of groundwater becomes more com-

---

[3]Bruce Beattie, "Irrigated Agriculture and the Great Plains: Problems and Policy Alternatives," *Western Journal of Agricultural Economics* 6 (December 1981): 291.

[4]"Depletion of Underground Water Formation."

petitive, close attention must be paid to the structure of property rights in the resource if efficient allocation is to result.

Before discussing groundwater rights, it is important to understand the basic physical characteristics of the resource. For the most part, groundwater does not flow in streams beneath the earth's surface nor do groundwater basins resemble lakes. The hydrology of groundwater is not so simple. Groundwater is stored in and transmitted through permeable underground rock formations whose boundaries are difficult to determine and whose degree of permeability varies as the formation changes. Where lateral movement of water is rapid, pumping at one location has a direct impact on the water table at another location. Where lateral movement is limited, however, pumping interdependencies are also limited, since water drawn at one location does not reduce water in another. Recharge of groundwater basins also varies. Where top soil is permeative, surface water quickly enters the aquifer. Clay layers, on the other hand, can prevent recharge and greatly reduce the flow in the basin.

From this simple discussion come two important considerations for groundwater rights. First, unlike surface water, groundwater can be stored without constructing large dams and without flooding valuable land. Aquifers provide a natural storage system that can be drawn down or built up depending on the rate of withdrawals relative to recharge. Second, since groundwater cannot be seen, it is difficult to measure the quantity and quality of the resource; and measurement is necessary for the definition, enforcement, and transfer of property rights. Fortunately, the science of groundwater hydrology has become more precise in recent years, making the definition and enforcement of rights to groundwater less costly. It is now possible to know with a great deal more certainty the direction and rate of groundwater flows. As pumping from groundwater basins increases, more data become available to help determine recharge, discharge, and permeability. With this information, the ability to define and enforce property rights in groundwater basins is greatly enhanced.

The Evolution of Groundwater Rights

The evolution of groundwater rights has followed a pattern similar to that of surface water rights. As long as groundwater was not scarce, it made little sense for the early American settlers to devote much effort to devising institutions to govern its allocation. As with many of our property institutions, English rules were the simplest to adopt; and the English Rule of Absolute Ownership was first used to establish property rights in water. The rule gave the overlying landowner complete freedom to allocate groundwater without liability. Precedent had been established in the case of *Acton* v. *Blundell* in 1843, with Lord Chief Justice Tindal giving the following opinion:

> [I]n the case of a well sunk by a propriator in his own land, the water which feeds it from a neighbouring soil does not flow openly in the sight of the neighbouring propriator, but through the veins of the earth beneath its surface; no man can tell what changes these underground sources have undergone in the progress of time. It may well be, that it is only yesterday's data, that they first took the course and direction which enabled them to supply the well: again, no propriator knows what portion of water is taken from beneath his own soil: how much he gives originally, or how much he transmits only, or how much he receives. . . .[5]

Since the hydrology of groundwater was unknown and unknowable to early English courts, they avoided the issue by classifying groundwater as property, giving it the same status as rocks or minerals on or under the land. As Frank Trelease has pointed out, "It was in the light of this scientific and judicial ignorance that the overlying landowner was given total dominion over his 'property,' that is, a free hand to do as he pleased with water he found within his land, without accountability for damage."[6] This form of property rights worked well as long as third party injuries were rare; that is, as long as groundwater was not scarce.

As the demand for water grew and individuals began to compete for water and land use, the English Rule of Absolute Ownership had to be modified. United States courts softened the English rule with the American Rule of Reasonable Use, under which overlying landowners had coequal rights to the groundwater subject to "reasonable" use. This concept is similar to the beneficial use requirements imposed on surface water allocation. The determination of reasonableness is primarily a judicial one and is related to the demand by adjacent landowners to the common supply. But this aspect of the reasonable use doctrine can create uncertainty in tenure, since the determination of reasonableness is subject to the whim of the court and can change in response to economic and social conditions. Uncertainty increased as water became

---

[5]*Acton* v. *Blundell*, 12 M. and W. 349, 152 Eng. Rep. 123, 123 (1843).

[6]Frank J. Trelease, "Developments on Groundwater Law," in *Advances in Groundwater "Mining" in the Southwestern States*, Z. A. Saleem, ed. (Minneapolis: American Water Resources Association, 1976), p. 272.

more scarce and as more uses were challenged as unreasonable. The challenges have produced varying answers on

> whether it is reasonable to (a) sell water, (b) use it on non-overlying land, or (c) use it outside the natural drainage basin.
>
> Answers may differ to those questions, depending on whether "reasonable use" focuses on reasonable use of land or of water, and whether the case involves the basin to which water would return if it were used on overlying land.
>
> More troublesome is a tendency to deny that it is reasonable to sell water. This relates to what may be thought of as the water mystique, that water is a God-given resource inappropriate to be bought and sold. Or to a notion that one may do, in his own non-pecuniary interest and at his neighbor's expense, what he may not do by way of commercial exploitation.[7]

Another variation on the absolute use doctrine took root in the California courts at the beginning of the 20th century. Since it was not possible for all overlying users to meet their demands during drought years, conflicts arose over identifying the absolute rights of the overlying landowners. Efforts to change the doctrine resulted in the Correlative Rights Doctrine, which differed from the reasonable use doctrine in two basic respects. First, if the demand for groundwater exceeds the supply, all overlying owners must reduce their use on a coequal basis. Second, where supplies are in excess of the reasonable needs of overlying landowners, water may be put to non-overlying uses.

Conflict could not be avoided as population grew. As with surface water, increasing demands led to the repudiation of the riparian doctrine and the introduction of the doctrine of prior appropriation in most Western states. Rather than tying water rights to land ownership, under the prior appropriations doctrine the water right is acquired by use. Use rights are usually granted by permit through application to a public agency and are defined in terms of the quantity of water that may be withdrawn, the types of use to which water may be put, and sometimes the dates when the water rights can be exercised. Appropriative rights are not limited to overlying use and are established on a first-in-time, first-in-right basis, with preference given to senior water rights holders. As a result, in times of short supply, junior water rights holders may be shut out altogether.

The groundwater doctrines that exist today have evolved as a result

---

[7]Charles E. Corker, *Groundwater Law, Management and Administration*, Legal Study no. 6 (Washington, D.C.: National Water Commission, October 21, 1971), p. 105.

of changes in the benefits and costs of defining and enforcing property rights. The arid Western states follow the appropriations doctrine, with California using the correlative doctrine as well. The more humid Eastern states allocate groundwater according to the principle of reasonableness. The differences between the East and West can be traced to the higher annual precipitation experienced in the East, providing little incentive to modify the original doctrines of absolute ownership and reasonable use. It is not surprising that as some Eastern states experience groundwater overdraft, they have begun to modify their laws to conform more closely to those adopted in the West.

While it is true that the changing relative scarcity of groundwater has led to efforts to establish and revise groundwater rights, it is not true that the efforts have resulted in an efficient institutional arrangement where property rights are enforced and transferable. Current institutions are deficient both in terms of tenure certainty and transferability. In California, for example, to correct for problems inherent in the correlative rights doctrine, the state Supreme Court ruled in favor of mutual prescription doctrine. Under this doctrine, a safe level of extraction is determined and a share of the rights is allocated to groundwater users in the basin on the basis of extraction rates prior to adjudication. Since the system eliminates part of the common pool problem, it reduces tenure uncertainty and allows transferability. In the 1975 court case, *City of Los Angeles* v. *City of San Fernando*, however, the California Supreme Court undermined the mutual prescription doctrine by partially reinstating the correlative rights doctrine.[8] Adjudicated rights prescribed to a private pumper were transferred to the city of Los Angeles on the grounds that rights could not be prescribed against public entities. The Court had effectively reduced the certainty of rights. In another instance, the adjudication of the Tehachapi Basin in Southern California resulted in a restriction on the transfer of prescriptive rights, reducing efficient allocation in the basin.[9]

Rights for many groundwater basins have never been defined and enforced. Where riparian rights dictate that absolute or reasonable use is granted to overlying landowners, the problems of the common pool are severe. These doctrines may be adequate for solid minerals, but

[8]*City of Los Angeles* v. *City of San Fernando,* 14 Cal. 3d 199, 537 P3d 1250, 123 Cal Reptr. 1 (1975).

[9]Terry L. Anderson, Oscar R. Burt, and David T. Fractor, "Privatizing Groundwater Basins: A Model and Its Application," in *Water Rights: Scarce Resource Allocation, Bureaucracy, and the Environment,* Terry L. Anderson, ed. (Cambridge, Mass.: Ballinger Press, 1983).

riparian rights for a migratory resource like groundwater establish a rule of capture. Under such conditions, landowners have little or no incentive to conserve; if they do not get the water, someone else will. Furthermore, since under the reasonable use doctrine the courts determine reasonableness, tenure can change at any time and owners can lose their apparent rights without any compensation. Similarly, the prior appropriations doctrine often follows the "use it or lose it" principle, whereby rights can be lost if they appear to be abandoned, which creates a negative incentive for conservation.

Restrictions on transferability also exist. In general, riparian rights cannot be used on nonriparian land; that is, the rights are tied to specific parcels of land. While there are exceptions,[10] the riparian doctrine does not generally allow for transferability and, hence, allocation by a price system. Where the reasonable use doctrine has allowed transfer of groundwater to other uses, the transfers are subject to bureaucratic or judicial review. The transfer of appropriative groundwater rights is also subject to a hierarchy of uses; and, in some cases, the transfer results in the loss of priority. While prior appropriation is suited to transferability, the doctrine as presently interpreted often imposes limitations that interfere with exchange. Fortunately, there is a potential for altering property institutions in ways that will make groundwater allocation more efficient.

Privatizing Groundwater Basins

A groundwater basin is like a bathtub filled with saturated, coarse sand with a stream of water flowing in (natural recharge) and with water being pumped from the porous medium. If pumping is equal to net natural recharge, the saturation level in the sand will be stable; otherwise, the level will rise or fall as the difference between recharge and pumping is positive or negative. In most basins, a rising level of saturation is generally not a problem; but it is possible that a rising water table could flood low lands, and the owners of those lands would bear some costs. Once total extraction exceeds the rate of recharge, however, external effects begin to arise in the form of higher pumping costs, salt water intrusion, or land subsidence. Heavy groundwater pumping in the San Joaquin Valley in California, for example, has caused an area the size of Connecticut to subside by as much as 30 feet in some places. Savannah, Georgia, has drawn so much water from its city wells that saltwater is slowly being drawn toward the city's aquifer.

[10]Ibid.

Three other problems are important for determining the behavior of individual pumpers. First, pumping more water from one well can create a cone of depression around it. When water is removed from the porous material around the well, differential pressures cause water to be drawn from adjacent areas toward the depression. If two wells are located close to one another, pumping at well A can draw water from well B, raising the pumping costs there. Second, as the level of a groundwater basin is drawn down, all pumpers face higher lift costs. The incentive, therefore, is to pump the water as rapidly as possible while the lift costs are low. Third, groundwater users who want to conserve water face the risk of not being able to get that water in the future. Water left in the aquifer will be available to all other pumpers, so there is no guarantee that it can be captured at a later date.

For the most part, net natural recharge for a basin is a random variable. Hydrological studies can measure recharge at any point in time, but they cannot accurately predict how the flow will change over time. Therefore, stocks in the groundwater basin play a dual role. First, they provide the physical basis for water to be used in production, particularly under conditions where water supplies fluctuate randomly. Second, they affect pumping costs, as higher stocks imply lower pumping costs and vice versa. The rate of extraction will be a function of the expected value of water in production and the expected costs of pumping. Even though diminishing returns are likely to place a limit on pumping rates, if pumping rates are expected to rise as others pump from the basin, any individual's rate of extraction is likely to be greater.

The problem in groundwater management is to induce individuals to pursue an optimal rate of extraction. If a basin were owned by a single individual, we would expect the rate of extraction to maximize the basin's net present value, taking into account the current and future value of stocks. The immediate value of stocks will be mainly a function of the value of water in production or consumption; the future value will be a function of the impact additional stocks have on pumping costs, spatial distribution, and insurance values. Pumping costs, of course, will be inversely related to the level of groundwater stocks; greater stocks will mean lower pumping costs. The stock value of groundwater will also decline with the spatial distribution. This phenomenon is easily understood when the walls of the aquifer are bowl-shaped; as the level of water declines, the surface area of the water table decreases, reducing the land surface overlying the groundwater. Wells on the old perimeter go dry and water must be transported.

Finally, groundwater stocks will have an insurance value, since they can be stored from year to year to offset surface water variability.

When a groundwater basin is held in common and pumping is uncontrolled, externalities will arise and the net value of the basin will not be maximized. If enough small pumping units each pump a small share of the total, each unit will ignore its effect on groundwater stocks. For each pumping unit, leaving stocks in the aquifer has little impact on the total level of stocks, and there is no guarantee that the conserved stocks could be captured in the future. In other words, groundwater is a fugitive resource that is valuable only when it is captured; and we can expect groundwater basins to be overexploited, like buffalo or whales.

There are, however, some mitigating aspects to the groundwater problem that are not found with many other natural resources. Water is costly to transport, so with uncontrolled pumping nearly all groundwater is used on land overlying the aquifers. In effect, when groundwater is applied to a fixed land base, diminishing returns are inevitable. Furthermore, if groundwater moves slowly within the basin, externalities are reduced. Recall that, once disturbed by pumping activity, water must move through porous media to reach an equilibrium. Insofar as the movement into an area being heavily pumped is slow, the externality is reduced. In some basins, lateral movement can take years.

Most economists have concluded that the problems with groundwater can only be overcome with central management, but there is evidence that a well-defined, easily enforced, and transferable set of rights can be established. Vernon Smith has proposed an innovative approach to the privatization of groundwater basins, using the Tucson Basin as an illustration.[11] Smith's scheme would issue a property deed for some amount of water to each individual water user i, $i = 1, 2 \ldots n$, for n users in total. The deeds would have two components, one allowing claim to a percentage of the basin flow and the other to a percentage of the stock. The property rights would be allocated to individuals in proportion to their pumping rates during some base period. Using the Tucson Basin and a base period of 1975, the individual proportions would be a function of total use, that is, 224,600 acre feet. If individual use was x_i acre feet, that individual's proportion of total use, P_i, would be $x_i/224,600$. Based on this proportion, P_i, each pumper would receive two rights:

[11]Vernon L. Smith, "Water Deeds: A Proposed Solution to the Water Valuation Problem," *Arizona Review* 26 (January 1977): 7–10.

1. The flow right would be based on a fraction of long-run average net natural recharge to the basin which is 74.6 thousand acre feet. Therefore, the property right of individual i to the annual recharge is $ri = 74.6 \, P_i$ thousand acre feet in perpetuity.

2. The second property deed would convey a right to a share of the basin's stock which was approximately 30 million acre feet in 1975. The share of this stock granted to individual i would also be P_i.[12]

The initial allocation of water rights is arbitrary and primarily a question of equity, and it can promote waste.[13] To assign the water deed using the appropriative doctrine usually means that potential claimants must show evidence of use, so users may race to the pump-house. To avoid the incentive to waste water in establishing a priority right, water deeds could be assigned to landowners in proportion to land overlying the aquifer. By allowing transferability, this method would ultimately achieve an economically efficient allocation.

Given some initial allocation of rights to the flow and stock components of groundwater, consider the operational accounting system for enforcement. Pumps would be metered, and each owner of a right would begin with an initial stock. At the end of each year, an adjustment would be made to the stock account by subtracting the amount pumped and adding the appropriate share of aggregate natural recharge. Since the latter component is a random variable, observed stream flows or other sources of recharge would be used to estimate recharge. If return flows from irrigation were of consequence, they would be applied to reduce the subtraction from pumping. A way to maintain the integrity of the meters would have to be devised, and violations for pumping water in excess of the amount owned would be handled with fines.

By assigning rights to flows and stocks and allowing transferability, efficiency can be improved. Transferability forces private decision-makers to consider the full opportunity costs of their actions and makes efficiency among different basins possible by allowing interbasin transfers. To protect third parties, who benefit from incidental recharge, interbasin transfers would have to be restricted to consumptive use. For example, if consumptive use were 65 percent, as it is in the Tehachapi Basin in California, a person who wants to transfer 130 acre feet out of the basin would have to relinquish his right to 200 acre feet. The remaining 70 acre feet (35 percent) would be left in the basin to provide

[12]Ibid., p. 8.

[13]See Terry L. Anderson and P. J. Hill, "Establishing Property Rights in Energy: Efficient v. Inefficient Processes," Cato Journal 1 (Spring 1981).

what would have been incidental recharge. In this way, transferability of private consumptive rights promotes efficient allocation.

Another important consideration for economic efficiency in an economy with random elements is the availability of markets in which risks can be shared among all producers and consumers. There must be an opportunity for the relatively more risk-averse parties to exchange with the relatively less risk-averse parties some "riskiness" for something else of value. When stocks are privately owned, this opportunity exists among all producers in the basin. The relatively risk-averse producer will hold more stocks than a less risk-averse producer as a contingency against water shortage associated with random fluctuations in recharge and demand. Equilibrium price and quantities of stocks held by producers will reflect differential risk preferences among the producers in the basin.

While the assignment of rights to stocks and flows improves efficiency with respect to exchange and risk, the property rights system does not completely solve the commonality problems associated with pumping costs and spatial distribution. An individual user may hold title to a certain stock of water, but the conditions under which the water can be obtained in the future are altered by the use rates of other users in the basin. First, rapid pumping in the aggregate will increase the future cost of pumping for any individual firm. Second, a firm that tends to conserve its stock of water relative to the aggregate may assume an additional risk if it is located near the perimeter of the aquifer, which might not be as deep as the center. The firm could find itself with title to a sizable stock but with no groundwater left under its land. Rights in that stock could be sold, but with a declining surface area of land overlying the remaining saturated part of the aquifer, the value of the stock would likely depreciate.

To achieve efficiency, given positive pumping costs or the spatial distribution externality or both, there must be a limited modification of the property rights scheme. When initial stocks are allocated to private owners, some stocks must be withheld from allocation to ensure that the water level in the basin does not fall too low. The ideal or equilibrium level of stocks to be withheld, however, is difficult to determine, since many of the hydrologic and economic variables are random and subjective. Improved information will be available after the initial appropriation of stocks for private property has been made; and, in an *ex post* sense, better estimates will evolve over time. Unless there are significant economic or hydrologic surprises, the economic costs of error and the choice of stocks withheld should be relatively small.

In the final analysis, the effectiveness of assigning private property rights to reduce withdrawal rates from a basin will depend on how firms interact under uncertainty. Assigning private rights would induce producers to pump somewhat less water than previously because stocks would have some pure inventory value. If producers extrapolate water table declines from experiences of uncontrolled pumping, observation of the new, more conservative behavior will generate expectations that pumping costs will increase less rapidly in the future than they have in the past. This expectation will encourage conservation and precipitate a revision of expected pumping costs. The slow evolution of pumping lifts over time provides plenty of opportunity for users to compare observations with expectations and thus make appropriate revisions. As long as pumpers follow this pattern, rates of withdrawal over time should not be too rapid.

The rate of use under private property rights will be closer to optimal if there are restrictions in lateral movements of groundwater stocks. With such restrictions, the pumping rate of the firm, as contrasted to all other firms in the aggregate, will impinge on the firm's future pumping costs and reduce the externality.

While the assignment of rights to stocks and flows may still leave some externality problems, far less central control would be required than with present systems. As many more decisions are placed in private hands, the information requirements for central control are reduced and the benefits and costs of decentralized decision-making are internalized. At least the pure inventory externality will be taken into account, and other sources of externality can be dealt with on the merits of their quantitative importance.

Private Rights in Practice

Assigning private, transferable rights to groundwater can potentially improve allocative efficiency, but do the potential gains justify the costs of establishing the rights? If the value of groundwater is low or if the cost of defining and enforcing rights is high, privatization is unlikely to occur. To date, most of the water literature has concluded that one or both of these conditions hold. Two exceptions, however, suggest that markets can play a greater role in groundwater allocation.

In 1973, Oklahoma enacted a law that provided for the assignment of transferable rights to groundwater. Under this law, groundwater basins can be dewatered as long as it takes place over a period of no less than 20 years. Rights to water in the basins are transferable, except when transfers are challenged by affected third parties, in which case the challenge is resolved by a process similar to that governing surface water rights.

Unfortunately, there are three problems with the Oklahoma law. First, before rights can be assigned, hydrologic studies must be completed to determine the amount of water in the basin. Such studies are costly and sometimes take years to complete. By 1981, only 6 of 150 basins in Oklahoma had been studied.[14] Second, the Oklahoma statute provides for the assignment of rights to stocks but does not allocate potential recharge. As a result, some of the valuable water in an aquifer is left unowned and subject to common pool problems. Third, Oklahoma groundwater use is subject to a beneficial use clause, limiting potential transfers and opening the door for rent seeking (see chapter V).

A better example of how privatization can improve groundwater allocation exists in the Tehachapi Basin, located in Kern County approximately 35 miles southwest of Bakersfield, California, and 100 miles north of Los Angeles. The 37-square-mile basin is the largest of three adjudicated basins in the area covered by the Tehachapi-Cummings County Water District.[15] Water in the basin is used primarily for agriculture, although there are municipal and industrial uses. The only source of natural recharge to the basin is precipitation in adjacent watersheds.

Groundwater use in excess of safe yield, or overdraft, began in the Tehachapi Basin in the 1930s following a steady increase in irrigated acreage.[16] By 1960, withdrawals exceeded recharge by 60 percent. The water level in the overall basin dropped by an average of 70 feet per year between 1951 and 1961, while the level around the city of Tehachapi fell 110 feet. During this period, groundwater storage in the valley fell by over 61,000 acre feet. From 1961 to 1968, the water table continued to drop an average of 3 feet per year. Consequently, pumping costs increased dramatically, and some wells ran dry. Fears that con-

[14]Richard Stroup and John Baden, *Natural Resources: Bureaucratic Myths and Environmental Management* (Cambridge, Mass.: Ballinger Press, 1983), chap. 6.

[15]The historical analysis is drawn largely from Tehachapi Soil Conservation District, *Tehachapi Project Report,* March 31, 1969; John M. Gates, "Repayment and Pricing in Water Policy: A Regional Economic Analysis with Particular Reference to the Tehachapi-Cummings County Water District" (Ph.D. diss., Department of Agricultural Economics, University of California at Berkeley, 1969); and Albert J. Lipson, *Efficient Water Use in California: The Evolution of Groundwater Management in Southern California,* 4-2387/2-CSA/RF (Washington, D.C.: The Rand Corporation, November 1978). I have benefited greatly from conversations with John Otto, Assistant Manager, Tehachapi-Cummings County Water District, Tehachapi, California.

[16]For a more detailed discussion, see Anderson, Burt, and Fractor.

tinued overdraft would seriously affect the agriculturally based economy brought about the formation of the Tehachapi-Cummings County Water District.

In 1965, a citizen advisory committee was formed to consider the options for managing the basin. The committee decided to bring in surface water from the state water project's California Aqueduct and to adjudicate groundwater water rights in the basin. Because the basin is situated at an elevation of 4,000 feet, importing surface water required a pipeline to lift aqueduct water over 3,400 feet. This made surface water far more costly than groundwater, which in turn made it unlikely that users would find substitutes for groundwater without some additional incentive.

Adjudication of the Tehachapi Basin offered the main hope for controlling overdraft. In 1966, suit was filed in Kern County Superior Court on behalf of the water district. The judgment, handed down five years later, followed the mutual prescription doctrine and limited total extraction to safe yield. The court determined that each party's base water rights were to be set at the highest average annual extraction rate over five consecutive years during any period after overdraft began. These rights totalled 8,250 acre feet for the basin; yield was estimated to be two-thirds of the base rights, or 5,500 acre feet. The court also ruled that users pumping less than their allocated amount could stockpile part of the excess for up to two years, but the amount stockpiled was limited to 25 percent of the allowed allocation.[17] The costs of adjudication totaled $300,000 for 100 users, or less than $55 per acre foot.

To encourage the use of imported surface water that became available in late 1973, an exchange pool was established. The pool allowed users located near the surface water to be reimbursed for the difference between surface water costs and average groundwater pumping costs. Suppose, for example, that surface water for agricultural use was priced at $100 per acre foot, and average groundwater pumping costs were $40 per acre foot.[18] If an individual not adjacent to the pipeline wanted to use surface water, the watermaster could allow him to pump groundwater in excess of his adjudicated right at a charge of $60 per acre foot.

[17]Justifications for this rule are that excessive stockpiling might cause the aquifer to fill up, thus impairing surface drainage; and if too many stockpiled rights are exercised at one time, there might not be enough water to satisfy all demands due to cones of depression.

[18]Note that the average pumping costs for groundwater are determined by the watermaster and applied to all participants in the exchange pool regardless of their actual pumping costs.

During the same period, a user adjoining the pipeline would be required to substitute an equivalent amount of surface water for groundwater. That user would be reimbursed for the difference between surface water and average groundwater pumping costs, or $60 per acre foot.

There are, however, two restrictions on the exchange of groundwater rights in the Tehachapi Basin. First, the Kern County Assessor has ruled that water rights severed from the land are subject to the same taxes as mineral rights. These prohibitive taxes mean that the exchange of groundwater has occurred only by sale of the overlying land or short-term leases. Second, the watermaster must approve of groundwater extraction at a location other than where the water right was developed. When a water right is leased by or sold to another party, the water is not physically transported; it is pumped from the lessee's or buyer's well, which may be in another part of the basin. The rationale for requiring watermaster approval is that a substantial number of transfers could cause adverse effects in the area where pumping is increased. Even though total pumping in the basin is limited to safe yield, the transfer of rights within the basin could create cones of depression and increase pumping costs for some users.

Two lessons can be learned from the adjudication of the Tehachapi Basin. First, rights to groundwater can be defined and enforced. While the Tehachapi adjudication involved only rights to recharge, the fact that water can be stockpiled suggests that definition and enforcement of rights to the groundwater stock are also feasible. Second, casual observations show that major externalities in the Tehachapi Basin have been eliminated through adjudication. Water levels are no longer declining; the upward pressure on pumping costs has been eliminated. The importation of surface water has provided incidental recharge, which in turn has increased the water table in some areas. The city of Tehachapi no longer rations water as it did during some periods prior to adjudication, and rising water tables have brought previously marginal wells into production.

While limited privatization of rights to recharge has produced some improvements, further decentralization and privatization could increase efficiency even more. Remaining problems are due to restrictions on stockpiling, the absence of rights to the groundwater stock, subsidies that distort the true cost of imported surface water, and constraints on the transfer of groundwater rights.

Eliminating the 25 percent limit on stockpiling would decentralize decisions and move the system toward a long-run equilibrium, since the limitation can generate a loss of water from the system. For example, if a farmer is entitled to 100 acre feet of groundwater and uses only 60 acre feet during the year, his allowable allocation for the next year will be 125 acre feet. Rights to only 25 of the 40 acre feet not used can be retained by the farmer. While the 15 acre feet are not lost in a physical sense, the right to use the water is (see line 3 of table 8). Restrictions on carryover only make sense if the basin is at or near capacity, when stockpiling would impair surface drainage. This is not the case in the Tehachapi Basin. Since surface water is much more costly than groundwater, there is no rationale for restricting carryover.

The property rights framework calls for assigning rights to groundwater stocks, but the Tehachapi adjudication included no such provision. While it is true that the safe yield limitation eliminates externalities from drawdown, the absence of rights to the stock means that valuable water will be locked up and left in the ground. While spatial distribution of wells and environmental problems probably would dictate withholding some portion of the stocks, it is difficult to justify locking up the entire resource. Just as a user is granted a perpetual right to a percentage of flow, that user could be given a right to a percentage of the stock. Since surface water for agriculture has been two or three

Table 8

GROUNDWATER SURPLUS AND SURFACE WATER IMPORTATION, TEHACHAPI BASIN, IN ACRE FEET

	1975	1976	1977	1978	1979	1980
Groundwater surplus (allocation minus use minus temporary transfers)	1318	945	1983	2122	1959	2000
Allowable carryover	959	771	1268	1397	1141	1193
Percentage of surplus water foregone	27.2%	18.4%	36.1%	34.2%	41.8%	40.4%
Imported water use Agricultural	4032	2311	1337	1284	1565	2167
Municipal and industrial	110	178	136	319	452	75

SOURCE: Terry L. Anderson, Oscar R. Burt, and David T. Fractor, "Privatizing Groundwater Basins," in *Water Rights: Scarce Resource Allocation, Bureaucracy, and the Environment,* Terry L. Anderson, ed. (Cambridge, Mass.: Ballinger Press, 1983).

times more expensive than groundwater (see table 9), efficiency could be improved by allowing the use of less expensive groundwater stocks.[19]

The efficiency gains implicit in the price differentials are understated to the extent that surface water delivery is heavily subsidized for most users. Although the 1981 cost of water from the state water project was approximately $18 per acre foot, lifting the water 3,425 feet into the Tehachapi Basin added over $350 to the cost per acre foot. Furthermore, only municipal and industrial users without leases were required to pay the full cost, giving a heavy· subsidy to agricultural users and inducing them to use too much surface water. Eliminating the subsidy would reduce the overall demand for water, and establishing pumping rights would encourage the use of a lower cost resource.

Finally, restrictions on the transfer of water rights have reduced the efficiency of the system. Requiring watermaster approval for the transfer of water rights to other locations within the basin imposes a significant restriction on the largest rights holders in the basins. For example, the Monolith Portland Cement Company held about 1,200 acre feet of rights in 1980; but in recent years, it has lost large quantities of water due to the carryover limitation. Since the company's rights are on the

Table 9

WATER CHARGES AND COSTS, TEHACHAPI BASIN, PER ACRE FOOT

	1978	1979	1980	1981
Surface Water				
Municipal and industrial				
No lease	$283	$299	$394	$440
One-year lease	$195	$201	$257	$279
Agricultural	$ 90	$ 95	$110	$121
Groundwater				
Average groundwater pumping costs	$ 32	$ 32	$ 46	$ 59
Ratio of imported agricultural water charge to groundwater costs	2.81	2.97	2.39	2.05

SOURCE: See table 8.

[19]It would be efficient to use groundwater instead of surface water as long as the cost of surface water is greater than the sum of groundwater pumping costs and user cost, which is the imputed value of a unit change in the groundwater stock.

east end of the basin and agricultural demands are on the west end, watermaster approval is necessary to effect transfers. Approval is not routinely granted, since it is believed that large-scale transfers to one location might create cones of depression and increase pumping lifts. In light of the quantity and value of water being lost, however, it would be worthwhile to determine whether cones of depression and increased costs are significant. Restrictions on transfer may prove to be an expensive solution to a small problem.

Summary

Approaches to groundwater allocation traditionally have begun with central management because of the assumption that the definition and enforcement of rights are infeasible. As the value of water rises, however, additional efforts will be devoted to obtaining the rental value of the water. Will these efforts be devoted to rent seeking from bureaucratic managers or to defining and enforcing rights that will encourage efficient, decentralized management? The evidence from Oklahoma and the Tehachapi Basin suggests that privatization has improved allocation at reasonable costs and that bureaucratic restrictions on pumping from stocks and on transfers continue to promote inefficiency. Establishing both stock and flow rights to groundwater has the potential for eliminating inefficiency and reducing centralized information requirements. As the scarcity of surface water and groundwater increases, privatizing the commons offers the best hope for getting the highest value from these resources.

VIII. Conflict or Cooperation in Future Water Policy?

The water crisis is an institutional crisis, and the rules of the game that determine the demand and supply of water have seriously distorted information and incentives. To correct the demand-side problems, most policies call for conservation programs that do not include price increases. To correct the supply-side problems, major storage and delivery systems are seen as the technological solution. Proposed solutions to the water crisis are no different than many political solutions that have been proposed to solve the energy crisis. We can be certain, however, that governmentally sponsored technological fixes will not relieve the symptoms or the causes of the water crisis.

Since the water crisis is an institutional problem, the solution must also be institutional. But instead of using collective action to find a technological solution, it is more productive to consider adopting alternative rules of the game that will induce water consumers to curtail their demands and private water producers to increase their supplies. Furthermore, the solution must be aimed at promoting cooperation rather than generating conflict. Under the present structure, conflict is epidemic. Consumers are asked to reduce demands in one region so that more water will be available in other regions. When municipalities run short of water and streams are fully claimed, the water is removed from other uses without paying the full opportunity costs. As Robert Reid has written, "When California needs more water, they take it from their neighbors."[1] Since the rights to instream uses are poorly defined, if they exist at all, conflict is inevitable. Pollution damages downstream users, and withdrawals reduce water availability for fishing, recreational, and other nonconsumptive uses.

As long as collective action dominates water allocation, one interest group's gain will be another's loss, and pie slicing will be the name of the game. By relying on markets, however, the game can be changed to encourage pie enlarging. As water consumers and producers search

[1]Robert L. Reid, "Making Deserts Bloom," *The Progressive* 45 (July 1981): 24.

for mutually beneficial trades, cooperation will replace conflict. Traders in a water market will have an incentive to work together to find mutually advantageous solutions. The issue is whether future water policy will maintain the status quo or move toward a market solution.

Federal Water Programs

At the federal level, there is reason to believe that government will continue to play a smaller role in the supply of water. Throughout the 1970s, the power of federal construction agencies declined, there were fewer new starts in water development programs, and a smaller share of the budget was allocated to water agencies. In 1950, the Bureau of Reclamation commanded 61 percent of the Department of Interior's budget; by 1980, the share had fallen to 14 percent. The Carter administration, backed by environmentalists, made some inroads into decreasing the federal government's dominance of water policy. To signal his determination to alter the mission of the Bureau of Reclamation, President Carter changed the bureau's name to the Water and Power Resource Service, indicating a shift from active governmental intervention to a managing, oversight role for the agency. Even though the change only lasted for three years, it was nevertheless symbolic of a growing belief that federal control of water is unwise. President Carter also compiled a water hit-list, containing 32 projects that received no budget and several others that were cut substantially. In addition, the Carter administration tightened the Principles and Standards of the Water Resources Council and its procedures for doing cost-benefit analysis, making the economic justification of water projects, especially irrigation projects, almost impossible. None of these efforts was well-received at the state level. Congress responded to the discontent by budgeting almost all of the projects on the original hit-list in an attempt to reinstate the dominance of the federal government.

The Reagan administration assumed power on a platform generally aimed at turning more resource allocation decisions over to the private market. In addition to the influence of the new administration's political philosophy, fiscal constraints have forced the federal government to continue curtailing large, expensive water projects. Nevertheless, the rhetoric of the water pork barrel, which began with the Reclamation Act of 1902, continues. Secretary of Interior James Watt, for example, has forecast a serious water crisis in the next decade because the federal government lacks the billions of dollars needed to solve the water problems. Even if the money were available, Watt said, "we don't have the political clout" to make the necessary improvements because House

112

committees are "made up of people who don't want to invest."[2] If the money were there, we are led to believe, the federal government would be pushing forward with large-scale water projects.

These fiscal constraints have combined with other policy changes to reduce federal involvement in water policy. Following the initiative of the Carter administration, the Reagan administration has attempted to place more of the financial burden for water projects on states. President Carter called for states to supply 10 percent of the initial funds for water projects with marketable outputs and 5 percent of initial funds for those with nonmarketable outputs. President Reagan has attempted to toughen the standards by introducing the National Water Resources Policy and Development Act in the Senate. The act would substantially increase state control and financial responsibility for water projects, requiring states to finance 25 percent of planning costs, 25 percent of construction costs, and 50 percent of operation and maintenance costs. These policies suggest that there is a tendency at the federal level to decentralize the financial responsibility and control of water resource development.

Another positive sign comes from water pricing policies at the Department of Interior. In the Westlands Water District in California, farmers are supposed to repay the government for water projects, but the Bureau of Reclamation has used "ability to pay" criteria to determine whether repayment should be forced; the result has been large water subsidies.

> Routinely, even the most successful of landowners are not found to have much ability when it comes to paying for the project. In the San Joaquin Valley, for instance, the Fraint-Kern Canal provides water for land owned by Getty Oil, Tenneco West, J. G. Boswell (a huge cotton corporation), and other prosperous companies. Their ability to pay for the water was calculated by the water district to be $3.50 per acre-foot—one-seventh of what even low-priced California state-project water costs.[3]

Secretary Watt, once an advocate for large landowners as head of the Mountain States Legal Foundation (see chapter V), is moving to eliminate the low prices by seeking a long-term contract with landowners in the Westlands district, which would raise prices from $7.50 to $13 per acre foot. The increase would still only make the price half that

[2]"Watt Forecasts Water Woes to Stir U.S. Crisis," *Denver Post*, August 13, 1982.

[3]Ronald Brownstein and Nina Easton, "The Wet, Wet West," *Washington Monthly* 13 (November 1981): 44–45.

charged for state-project water, but it is a step toward establishing a market clearing price. While charging higher prices and distributing smaller subsidies are certainly encouraging signs, it remains to be seen whether the political climate will continue to keep the Army Corps of Engineers and the Bureau of Reclamation from engaging in large water projects and direct water allocation.

Can States Do Better?

As the federal government becomes less involved in water policy, states have been assuming a larger role. Trends in water institutions at the state level, however, do not necessarily indicate further decentralization. The "fear and loathing of the marketplace"[4] has most recently been expressed in California in the form of Proposition 13, which would drastically change the California water system. Fortunately, the initiative was defeated on November 2, 1982, but the thinking it reflected hardly suggests that policymakers are seriously considering market alternatives.

Proposition 13 contained four main components, only one of which was consistent with a market solution to the water crisis. According to the initiative, every water district in the state, including those responsible for water allocation in major metropolitan areas, would have to submit programs for water conservation to the Water Resources Control Board by January 1, 1985. The plans would specify how each district could hold down the rate of growth in its demands for water. The Water Resources Control Board would then have to approve each district's plan and would have the power to withhold any new or increased water supplies from state water projects until an acceptable plan was submitted. Even though this provision focused on the demand side of the water crisis, it incorporated no market incentives and created more possibilities for rent seeking. With so much power residing in the Water Resources Control Board, water districts would have to expend a great deal of effort convincing the board of the merits of their conservation programs, and costly administrative and judicial processes would be the result.

The initiative also required the establishment of water management agencies in 11 critical groundwater basin areas within a year. The agencies would be responsible for establishing and implementing a

[4]Timothy D. Tregarthen, "Water in Colorado: Fear and Loathing of the Marketplace," in *Water Rights: Scarce Resource Allocation, Bureaucracy, and the Environment*, Terry L. Anderson, ed. (Cambridge, Mass.: Ballinger Press, 1983).

groundwater management program designed to reverse the over-pumping in most basins. With overdraft in the state estimated at 2.2 million acre feet, there is definitely a need for improving groundwater allocation, but this requirement did not include any provision for the establishment of property rights or markets. The plans would have to be approved by the Water Resources Control Board, and the board would be able to stop state water project transfers and deny permission for increased pumping from new or existing wells. Again, the possibility for solving problems through the cooperation of the marketplace was to be replaced with the conflict inherent in the rent-seeking process.

Since existing California law does not permit groups to request the Water Resources Control Board to preserve water for instream uses, Proposition 13 allowed environmental, fishing, and recreational groups to petition the board for stream protection. Under existing law, such groups must await a diversion request and then protest its approval. Proposition 13 would have given instream users an offensive as well as a defensive position. While such a move would have improved the existing system, it still did not recognize that the basic problem is the inability of people to define and enforce rights to instream flows. The market solution would apply perfectly to this problem, but it was not being considered.

Finally, Proposition 13 would restrict the Bureau of Reclamation from filling the New Malones Reservoir until 75 percent of the project's water had been contracted for and would increase the price of that water dramatically. This provision seemed to be part of the growing recognition that cheap federal water has encouraged waste and environmental destruction. By requiring that water users pay the cost of water projects and the opportunity cost of water, this part of Proposition 13 would have moved water policy in the direction of a market solution. While there are definite legal questions as to whether the state can place restrictions on federal projects, this provision suggested that some people do understand that a water market would not allow such massive water subsidies.

In spite of this last provision, Proposition 13 was basically calling for an institutional change that would have increased the role of politics in water allocation. All of the problems addressed in Proposition 13 could be handled with property rights and the market solutions described in this book. Unfortunately, most politicians and bureaucrats are not interested in market solutions; they are interested in maintaining their power over water allocation decisions. Because we have ignored for so long the potential for market solutions and encouraged rent seeking through the political process, little attention is now being given to decentralized allocation mechanisms. In short, a market solution to the water crisis does not appear to be forthcoming in California, a state continually on the edge of a water crisis.

The extent to which states have political mechanisms designed to allocate water is shown in figure 4. Most states have some form of comprehensive water planning in place, and the power granted to planning agencies varies considerably from state to state. Nonetheless, it is clear that most states use a political mechanism to allocate water, precluding market allocation. Without significant funding for constructing new water projects, state planning agencies will have to confine themselves to allocation decisions over existing water supplies. The political game will no longer be played in terms of who gets funding for projects; it will determine how existing water is allocated. With federal influence greatly reduced, influence will simply be shifted to the state capitals, where the possibility for market allocation receives little more attention.

An Emerging Coalition

The real problem in effecting institutional change is in getting from here to there. There is little hope that politicians living in a rent-seeking society will actively support the decentralization of water policy. Politicians and bureaucrats currently work within a system that gives them the discretionary power necessary to reward their constituencies. If the coalition between politicians/bureaucrats and water users is to be opposed, the opposition must come in the form of a competing coalition.

The evidence and arguments presented in this book suggest the possibility for such a coalition among environmentalists, fiscal conservatives, and persons who value individual freedom. While this coalition would have been impossible a few years ago, there is growing evidence that these groups may have found some common ground. In recent debate in California over the Peripheral Canal initiative, for example, the Environmental Defense Fund (EDF) found itself aligned with urban residents in the Bay Area, farmers, and large businesses in Northern California who feared having their water taken for use in Southern California. Thomas J. Graff, general counsel for the EDF asked: "Has all future water-project development been choked off by the new conservationist-conservative alliance . . . ?" He went on to examine the moral premises for the coalition:

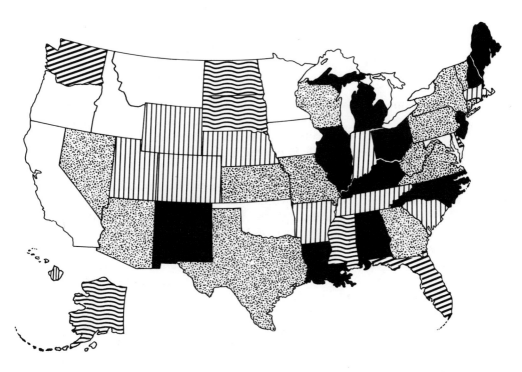

Figure 4
STATE STATUTORY AUTHORITY FOR WATER RESOURCES PLANNING AND MANAGEMENT

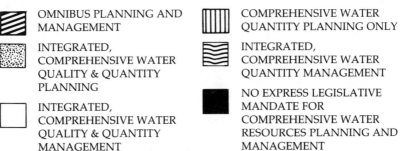

OMNIBUS PLANNING AND MANAGEMENT

INTEGRATED, COMPREHENSIVE WATER QUALITY & QUANTITY PLANNING

INTEGRATED, COMPREHENSIVE WATER QUALITY & QUANTITY MANAGEMENT

COMPREHENSIVE WATER QUANTITY PLANNING ONLY

INTEGRATED, COMPREHENSIVE WATER QUANTITY MANAGEMENT

NO EXPRESS LEGISLATIVE MANDATE FOR COMPREHENSIVE WATER RESOURCES PLANNING AND MANAGEMENT

SOURCE: Kenneth Rubin, "The Capacity of States to Manage Water Resources Given a Decreased Federal Role," prepared for Symposium on Unified River Basin Management, Stage II, October 6, 1981.

117

Budget director David A. Stockman last year described the moral premise underlying the attempt by "new conservatives" to shrink government as follows: "We are interested in curtailing weak claims rather than weak clients. . . . We have to show that we are willing to attack powerful clients with weak claims. I think that's critical to our success." The moral premises of conservationists, as they joined liberals and conservatives to sink Proposition 9 [the Peripheral Canal Project], were not inconsistent with the new conservative doctrine. Conservationists believe that the water-development sector of development can shrink without harming anyone, weak or powerful, and that more efficiency would benefit the environment as well.[5]

On the same premises, the EDF attempted to join James Watt in his efforts to increase water prices in the Westlands Water District. Secretary Watt rejected EDF's offer to join him in the battle, but it is noteworthy that these old rivals found themselves on the same side of the issue.

The Nature Conservancy is also finding common ground with individuals and groups that many would consider environmental suspects. The Conservancy has 180 corporate members, each paying $1,000 in annual dues. With such companies as International Paper, Union Camp, Georgia Pacific, Anaconda Copper, and Gulf Oil on their side, The Nature Conservancy has consummated more than 2,000 land deals involving over one million acres. Peter Seligman, director of the California Nature Conservancy, has said that "the supporters . . . run from left to right. . . . some of them are conservative and some of them have long beards and live in the woods in Mendocino County."[6] By working through the market system with well-defined and enforced property rights, The Nature Conservancy has been able to accomplish its environmental goals in an atmosphere of cooperation. While its efforts have been aimed mainly at land where property rights are well-defined and enforced, the tactics would be no less applicable to water if water rights were clearly established.

Writing for *Progressive* magazine, Judith Randall described our current water system as an example of "robbing Peter to pay Paul." She noted that

> when push doesn't come to shove, there is almost no incentive to conserve. . . .
> The result is that tens of billions of Federal dollars have been invested

[5]Thomas J. Graff, "Future Water Plans Need a Trickle-Up Economizing," *Los Angeles Times*, June 14, 1982, p. V-2.

[6]"Group Trying to Save Grasslands," Bozeman, Mont. *Daily Chronicle*, October 26, 1982.

in dams and canals and that—while the rest of the country continues to pay disproportionately for this extravagance—the west is clamoring for more projects, to the tune of still more billions, because it is wantonly "mining" water from underground sources faster than it can be replaced.

More money is not the answer to this problem. An end to the pork-barrel of Peter by Paul is. Western water is a commodity needlessly scarce because it is vastly underpriced.[7]

As more people recognize that water policies are examples of robbing Peter to pay Paul, general taxpayers and fiscal conservatives will find it easier to side with environmentalists.

Writing in *The Nation*, Fred Powledge quoted the U.S. Geological Survey and alluded to the difficulty of accepting a market solution:

As increases in water use deplete the easily developable supplies, more costly additional supplies are being sought. As the costs of water go up, water resources become more and more like other economic commodities for which there are supplies, demands and a pricing and marketing structure to balance the supplies and demands.

It is not an idea that is easy for the humanistic-minded to like, for it conjures up highly likely images of the wrong people being in control of the economics of a substance that is absolutely essential to life. . . . The opportunities for corruption, abuse and political and economic capital are unlimited.[8]

Though the idea of using markets may not be easy for the humanistic-minded to accept, those same people are beginning to realize that "corruption, abuse and political and economic capital" run rampant in the current political system. The market may not be perfect, but it does offer an alternative capable of solving problems through cooperation between individuals and groups with diverse interests.

The foundation for an environmentalist/fiscal conservative alliance can be illustrated by the Tennessee Valley Authority (TVA) project on the Little Tennessee River. In 1936, the TVA proposed a dam on the lower Little Tennessee River, a project that was eventually introduced in 1963 as the Tellico Dam project. As with most dam construction, the opportunity cost of land, free-flowing water, and environmental disruption led those who would bear these costs to oppose the project. Nevertheless, Congress approved the funds for the Tellico project in 1966, and construction began in 1967; but the project was halted in 1971

[7]Judith Randall, "Robbing Peter to Pay Paul," *Progressive* 45 (July 1981): 26.
[8]Fred Powledge, "Water, Water, Running Out," *The Nation* 234 (June 1982): 715.

by a court injunction that required the TVA to file an environmental impact statement in compliance with the National Environmental Policy Act of 1969. When the environmental impact statement was filed, it showed a favorable benefit to cost ratio of 1.7:1, using a discount rate of 3.25 percent. Construction was resumed in 1973 and continued until 1977, when again it was halted by a court injunction based on the Endangered Species Act and the potential elimination of the snail darter.

The ensuing controversy produced another cost-benefit analysis by the TVA and the Department of Interior in 1978. Recognizing that the 3.25 percent discount rate was unrealistic, the 1978 cost-benefit analysis used a discount rate of 6.625 percent. Between 1971 and 1978, the energy crisis had forced electricity prices to rise and greatly increased the hydroelectric benefits from the dam. Annual benefits from the dam estimated in 1978 were over 30 percent greater than those estimated in 1971. At the same time, construction costs had increased even more dramatically, by more than 330 percent. The net result was a 1978 benefit to cost ratio of 0.5:1. By TVA's own admission, the Tellico Dam project was not economically justifiable. Nevertheless, the dam was built.

Fiscal conservatives are continually searching for examples of government projects with benefit to cost ratios less than one, and environmentalists are continually searching for private and public projects that have disastrous environmental consequences. When fiscal conservatives and environmentalists recognize that many federal water projects have both of the characteristics they disdain, it will be difficult to prevent a coalition from forming to fight current water policy.

In their introduction to *Bureaucracy vs. Environment*, John Baden and Richard Stroup discussed who would stand to benefit from constraints on excessive governmental action:

> Obviously, the general taxpayer benefits if the government operates in a manner consistent with economic efficiency. Environmentalists should welcome a reduction of governmental programs that failed to meet the tests of economic efficiency and are demonstrably destructive of the environment. . . . A third category of those likely to support careful analysis of governmental action are those who view freedom as a scarce and valuable resource and who realize that the growth of government, whatever the benefits, constitutes an extraordinarily serious, pervasive, and unavoidable threat to that resource.[9]

[9]John Baden and Richard Stroup, eds., *Bureaucracy vs. Environment* (Ann Arbor: University of Michigan Press, 1981), p. 7.

While Baden and Stroup were referring to many aspects of governmental intervention in natural resource allocation, their comments are no less applicable to water policy. Once a coalition of these three groups comes to recognize the mutual ground for their various interests, decentralization of water allocation is more likely to occur.

Thus, we return to the position taken by Jack Hirshleifer, James DeHaven, and Jerome Milliman quoted in chapter I:

> Other things being equal, we prefer local to state authority, state to federal—and private decision-making (the extreme of decentralization) to any of these. Our fundamental reason for this preference is the belief that the cause of human liberty is best served by a minimum of governmental compulsion and that, if compulsion is necessary, local and decentralized authority is more acceptable than dictation from a remote centralized source of power. This is an "extra market value" for which we at least would be willing to make some sacrifices in terms of loss of economic efficiency. . . . even on grounds of efficiency, however, we have some faith that, the more nearly the costs and benefits of water projects are brought to those who make decisions, the more correct those decisions are likely to be—a consideration which argues for decentralization in practice.[10]

By understanding the potential for market allocation of water resources and the potential for governmental failure in the allocation of those same resources, the potential exists for resolving our institutional water crisis. With more reliance on markets, it is possible to have less environmental destruction of water resources, more economic growth, and more individual freedom. If a coalition can be formed with an understanding of these potential gains, there is hope for averting the water crisis.

---

[10]Jack Hirshleifer, James DeHaven, and Jerome Milliman, *Water Supply: Economics, Technology, and Policy* (Chicago: University of Chicago Press, 1960), pp. 361–62.

ABOUT THE AUTHOR

Terry L. Anderson is professor of economics at Montana State University and an associate of the Center for Political Economy and Natural Resources. This year he is a visiting scholar at Oxford University in England and the University of Basel in Switzerland. Professor Anderson received his degrees from the University of Montana and the University of Washington and has served as a National Fellow at the Hoover Institution, Stanford University. He is the co-author of *Growth and Welfare in the American Past* (with Douglass C. North and P. J. Hill), editor of *Water Rights: Scarce Resource Allocation, Bureaucracy, and the Environment*, co-author of two other books, and author of numerous articles on economics and natural resources. He serves as Executive Director of the Montana Council on Economic Education.